Dealing with household emergencies

a Consumer Publication

Consumers' Association
publishers of **Which?**
14 Buckingham Street
London WC2N 6DS

a Consumer Publication

edited by   Edith Rudinger

published by   Consumers' Association
publishers of **Which?**

Consumer Publications
are available from
Consumers' Association
and from booksellers.
Details are given at
the end of this book.

ISBN 0 85202 206 9
and 0 340 25909 4

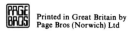
Printed in Great Britain by
Page Bros (Norwich) Ltd

Contents

Foreword

Reading this book will not turn anyone into an instant handyman, but will help the ordinary not-too-practical person to cope with urgent, relatively straightforward jobs. It does not attempt to advise on general maintenance and upkeep, but goes straight to the state of emergency that occurs, whether due to neglect or just bad luck.

The experienced and enthusiastic do-it-yourselfer generally already knows what to do and can recognise danger signs; others need to be warned when more skilful or hazardous jobs to do with electricity, gas or water, should be left to the expert or professional.

Read this book now, and be ready to put it into practice – hoping that these, or other, emergencies will not arise in your household.

Knowing where to turn

Go round your house or flat and make sure you know where the crucial turn-off points are for water, gas, electricity. Also be sure you know where the water tanks and cisterns are, including the one for the central heating system. Look for and note where the outside drains run, and where the manholes are.

Ideally, when you have located the essential points, write down or make a sketch where each is and pin up the note in a sensible place so that anybody in the house can find it when the need arises.

water

The external stop valve (which is the property of the water undertaking) is in an underground chamber, covered by a hinged lid. It is usually situated in the pavement outside the building, in a forecourt or just inside the garden. Turning this stop valve clockwise should stop all water flowing into the system. It may also cut off the water supply to your neighbours' premises (if so, you should warn your neighbours whenever you have to turn it off).

If the outside stop valve does not work properly, contact the water undertaking and have it put right: you may need to turn it off in a hurry. Keep a turn-key handy for turning it off – but you should only do so as a last resort in an emergency.

Locate, identify and label all stop valves inside your premises, if necessary with the help of a plumber.

Somewhere inside the building, usually in the kitchen or bathroom or underneath the stairs, or in the cellar, is another stop valve on the service pipe from the main supply (the rising main). Turning this stop valve will cut off the supply of cold water to the kitchen sink and may also turn off the supply to all other cold water taps and to the w.c. cistern. Or there may be another stop valve somewhere on the pipe distributing the water to the bath, wash basins and w.c. from the storage cistern in the loft or roof space.

If you discover that you have not got a main water stop valve within your own premises, it may be possible to have one inserted to give you control of your own water supply. This is particularly worth consideration if you share a building – if you live in a flat, for example, or in rented accommodation. Contact your local water undertaking to get an estimate of what this would involve.

In most modern houses and flats, there are usually drain cocks (with a spout) through which you can empty the water system with a hose pipe. There is normally a drain cock immediately above the main internal stop valve, and others may be on parts of the system that cannot be completely drained by opening taps.

In most houses, the hot water supply comes from a hot water cylinder which is supplied by the storage cistern. The pipe to the hot water taps leads off the top of the hot water cylinder. The cold water feed pipe, connected to the bottom of the cylinder to replace the hot water that is drawn from the taps, normally also has a stop valve.

A central heating system is generally replenished from a separate storage cistern in the roof space, with a stop valve on the supply pipe at each radiator and a drain cock at the boiler or the lowest part of the system.

electricity

The switch for turning off all the electricity to your premises is usually near the meter in what is now called the consumer unit (traditionally referred to as the fuse box). Here, too, are the main fuses or circuit breakers for the circuits in the house. Keep the box or cupboard enclosing the main switch and fuses clear of lumber and junk, because you may need to get at them in a hurry, or in the dark.

If the fuses are not already identified on a chart in the consumer unit, try the circuit fuses one by one to identify what part or parts of the home they affect. First, switch off the main switch. Then remove one fuse, switch on, and see what now does not work. Do this for each fuse in turn. Mark the fuse chart accordingly or put an explanatory list near the fuses (stick it inside the box, if feasible). All fuse holders are likely to be warm to the touch when they are in use, but if you find any of the fuse holders hot to the touch, there is a fault somewhere and you should call in a qualified electrician to investigate.

Keep a supply of the appropriate cartridge fuses or fuse wire near the main fuses. Put a torch there permanently ready for use, preferably one that can be stood up on its own and is adjustable so that it can throw a beam on your work when you have to replace fuses in the dark. Remember to check it regularly to make sure it is still functioning – batteries have a nasty habit of being flat just when you need them. Candles and matches would be an alternative, but they can be accidentally dropped or knocked over (or prove too much of a temptation to children) and cause a fire.

gas

The tap for turning on and off the main gas supply may be at the meter or very close to it. (Do not remove the key handle from its spigot). Unlike a valve, it does not have a gradual action: a quarter turn (through 90°) rotary movement is all that is required to change from 'on' to 'off' or vice versa. If you are not certain that you know which way to move the handle for 'on' or 'off', ask the meter reader the next time that he or she calls. If the tap is stiff and will not turn properly, do not force it. Call the local gas service centre who will send someone to loosen it (free of charge).

A leaflet published by British Gas *Help yourself to gas safety* tells you

How to turn off the main gas supply:
First, turn off all appliance taps and pilot lights. Then turn the main gas tap to the 'off' position. It is off when the notched line on the spindle of the tap points *across* the pipe.

How to turn on again:
Ensure that all appliance taps and pilot lights are turned off. Then simply return the main gas tap to the 'on' position. It is on when the notched line on the spindle lies *along* the pipe. Then relight all the pilot lights on all your appliances.

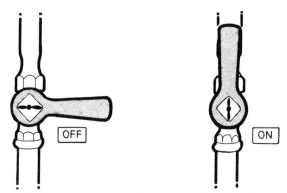

Remember to check when you turn the gas back on again that no tap was left turned on, before you re-light any pilot lights. A little time may elapse between turning on the main gas and being able to light and use pilot lights.

The leaflet goes on to say that

If you smell gas
The actions you must take immediately are:
1 Put out cigarettes. Do not use matches or naked flames.
2 Do not operate electrical switches (including doorbells).
3 Open doors and windows, to get rid of the gas.
4 Check to see if a tap has been left on accidentally, or if a pilot light has gone out.
5 If not, there is probably a gas leak. So turn off the whole supply at the meter and call gas service. The telephone number to call is under 'gas' in the directory.
6 If you cannot turn off the supply, or the smell continues after you have, or if you have no supply, you *must* call gas service or ask someone else to do so.

If a tap has not been left on accidentally and the smell goes after you have turned off the supply, there is probably a gas leak from the pipes in your premises. This should be repaired by a competent person and you must not turn the gas on again until the repair is completed.

Be specially alert when returning to buildings which have been left vacant for some time.

drains

The downpipes running from the roof gutter to ground level are rainwater pipes. The pipes may go straight into the ground or out into a gully. It can be difficult to establish where the rainwater flows from there onwards: it may be into the main drainage system or into a soakaway (an underground pit filled with rubble). A soakaway will be some distance from the building and covered with topsoil so that it is generally difficult to locate.

Other types of pipe can be identified by tracing them to their sources, such as sink, bath and basins. Waste water from these is generally carried in 1½ to 2-inch diameter vertical or inclined pipes outside the building, or shares the 4-inch diameter soil pipe leading from a lavatory. In houses built since 1966, soil pipes from lavatories are inside the building, usually boxed in by some removable covering, running vertically though the house. A 4-inch vertical pipe outside, running to the top of the building, is for ventilation purposes. In older houses, the soil pipe from a lavatory comes through the external wall of the house and connects to the ventilation pipe outside.

Domestic drains have inspection chambers (manholes – access points to the sewerage system) at junctions and other strategic points, primarily for rodding to clear obstructions. You can tell where an inspection chamber is by its round or rectangular cover set into the ground. If you take the cover off, you may be able to see which drains run into it by turning likely taps or flushing the lavatory. In some cases, a rainwater pipe and a waste pipe from the house both discharge into the same chamber.

A detached or semi-detached house is more likely to have its own set of drains connecting to the public sewer. Most local authorities keep plans which show the drains on properties in the district, and from one of these it should be possible to ascertain the layout of drains on a particular property and where they go.

On terraced houses, and on some other closely spaced properties, the drains from each property often run into a communal drain at the rear of the group of houses and then, at the end of the group, connect to the public sewer.

Drainage systems shared by neighbouring properties may have common inspection chambers.

If the manhole is on your neighbours' land, make their acquaintance and come to some arrangement with them about access, for when you need it. You probably have a right of access to a common manhole but it is better to have an amicable understanding between you.

If you think your manhole is unsightly, do not be tempted to bury it under a rockery or hide it under a big tub which, when filled with soil, will be wellnigh irremovable. If you must disguise it, use something light. A couple of sprigs of *cotoneaster horizontalis* planted close beside it and a bit of *sedum* (stonecrop) near the edges will clothe it without making for future problems.

In areas remote from a public sewerage system, house drains may lead to a cesspool or septic tank system located in a remote part of the garden or plot. If your foul water disposal is by cesspool or septic tank, do not put anything irremovable over the lid or cover.

A cesspool is generally just a lined hole in the ground where sewage collects. To prevent overflowing when full, it needs to be emptied; this is usually carried out on a regular basis by the local authority, for a charge. A septic tank is similar but should have a suitable filter or land drainage system attached. It does not need such frequent emptying because breakdown of the sewage occurs by bacterial action. Only the remaining solid matter in a holding tank needs to be removed, normally once a year.

who to call on

Make a list of the names, telephone numbers and addresses of service departments, tradesmen, repairers and other sources of emergency help to call on when needed. As well as firms and people you have yourself already used, and those recommended to you by neighbours or friends, cut out from local newspapers or magazines the advertisements of useful-sounding firms and individuals in the repair business. The list should include:

builders(s)
central heating engineer
chimney sweep
doctor
electrician(s)
electricity board service department
fire brigade ('999' and local fire station)

gas fitter(s)
gas region service centre/'gas escapes'
glazier(s)
local authority environmental health/engineer's department
locksmith
neighbour(s)
odd-job man
plumber(s)
police ('999' and local station)
service agent for dishwasher, freezer, tv set, washing machine
taxi or radio cab
tool hire firm
veterinary surgeon
water undertaking

Keep the list always in the same place, so that you or others in the household do not have to waste time desperately looking for it when the need arises.

Make a note of how satisfied you were with those you have used, and what their charges were, and the date. Discard any who were not satisfactory or failed to turn up or made an exorbitant charge.

responsible bodies

The Electrical Association for Women (25 Foubert's Place, London W1V 2AL) exists to give advice, information and practical instruction on the safe and efficient use of electricity in the home. It has branches throughout England, Scotland and Wales, and runs day courses for members of the public (including men) on how to wire plugs, replace fuses, read the meter, and on electrical appliances generally. It publishes a journal, and issues leaflets and booklets on various aspects of electricity and its uses, and has a display room in London where information and advice can be obtained.

Some trades have professional associations or organisations whose members have to comply with certain standards. It is sensible to use firms or individuals who are members of such bodies.

for plumbing
A plumber who is registered with the Institute of Plumbing has to

satisfy the Institute that he will carry out work competently and responsibly, and conform to water by-laws and building regulations.

The Institute of Plumbing's *Business directory of registered plumbers* is available in public libraries and in the offices of water undertakings. A list of registered plumbers in your area can also be obtained on request either by telephone (Hornchurch 51236) or by sending a stamped self-addressed envelope to The Institute of Plumbing, Scottish Mutual House, North Street, Hornchurch, Essex RM11 1RU. The Institute issues a leaflet *Plumbing in the home: advice to householders*, and one called *Get to know a plumber*. The leaflets are free; send a stamped self-addressed envelope.

The members of the Scottish and Northern Ireland Plumbing Employers' Federation (2 Walker Street, Edinburgh EH3 7LB) are firms of contractors, including single-man businesses, engaged in plumbing and mechanical services. Members have to satisfy certain entry requirements and are organised by local associations, who can supply names and addresses of member firms in any area.

for gas
To get a qualified repairer for a gas appliance or installation, ask at the gas showrooms to see a copy of the CORGI register, or ask the citizens advice bureau. CORGI stands for the Confederation for the Registration of Gas Installers (St Martin's House, 140 Tottenham Court Road, London W1P 9LN; telephone 01-387 9185). The register gives the names, addresses and telephone numbers of registered installers, in town order, together with information of the type of work undertaken.

for electrical work
The National Inspection Council for Electrical Installation Contracting (NICEIC), 237 Kennington Lane, London SE11 5QJ (telephone 01-582 7746) publishes annually a roll of approved electrical contractors who have undertaken to comply with the regulations for the electrical equipment of buildings, and whose work is subject to regular inspection by the NICEIC.

The list also indicates approved contractors who are members of the Electrical Contractors' Association (ECA) and covered by the ECA's customer protection guarantee scheme.

for domestic appliances

Three organisations representing many manufacturers and retailers of electrical goods have codes of practice: The Association of Manufacturers of Domestic Electrical Appliances (AMDEA), The Electricity Council, The Radio Electrical and Television Retailers' Association (RETRA). The codes are mainly concerned with arrangements for servicing and repairs, and include the requirement that when you telephone or write for help, you will normally be offered a service visit within 3 working days, that in most cases the repair should be completed during the first visit, that you should be advised of any minimum charge and, on request, be given an estimate of the cost of the work needed and advised whether the estimate is free, that the spare parts most frequently needed should be kept in stock at all times. If you call on a firm or service agent who is a member of one of these bodies and do not get satisfactory service, you can complain to the head office:

AMDEA, 593 Hitchin Road, Stopsley, Luton, Bedfordshire LU2 7UN
RETRA, 57–61 Newington Causeway, London SE1 6BE
The Electricity Council, 30 Millbank, London SW1P 4RD (or the headquarters of your area electricity board).

Some manufacturers and suppliers franchise a separate or subsidiary organisation to deal with the after-sales work for them. You should make a point of finding out who the firm or agent is to turn to for any work needed under the guarantee and for future service. It is better to know who the properly accredited agent is rather than to risk having to call in some 'any model, any time' repairer who may use non-standard parts or makeshift bits and pieces.

Most of the larger manufacturers and suppliers offer renewable service contracts for a fee. This generally includes one annual routine visit and any servicing required, without charging for labour costs or, with some, for any spare parts needed. Some manufacturers refuse to renew maintenance contracts when the machine gets too old (when it becomes a bad risk). This may be after as little as four or five years.

Most manufacturers produce service manuals to tell servicemen how to repair an appliance. Some of these manuals explain how the appliance works, how to take it apart (and put it back together again) and how to find out what is wrong and how to put it right. For electrical appliances, these manuals usually comprise wiring and component diagrams. Most laymen would have difficulty in understanding them (nor have the necessary special tools). But for a less usual or foreign model, it might be useful to the repairer you call in. Not all manufacturers are prepared to supply manuals to individuals (and when they do, it could be costly) but in special cases it may be worth asking for one.

for central heating installations
The Heating and Ventilating Contractors' Association runs a 24-hour answering service (01-229 5543) to provide the names of firms in any area who are members of the HVCA. The HVCA address is ESCA House, 34 Palace Court, London W2 4JG.

A list, in geographical regions, of members of the National Association of Plumbing, Heating and Mechanical Services Contractors in England and Wales is available from the Association at 6 Gate Street, London WC2A 3HX.

The Scottish and Northern Ireland Plumbing Employers' Federation (2 Walker Street, Edinburgh EH3 7LB) is the comparable body for Scotland and Northern Ireland.

for glazing
The Glass and Glazing Federation (6 Mount Row, London W1Y 6DY) will send a list of member companies in a particular area on request by telephone (01-409 0545) or letter. The list shows what products and services each firm can provide.

In Scotland, a list of members of the Scottish Glass Merchants and Glaziers Association is available from 13 Woodside Crescent, Glasgow G3 7UP.

for locks
If you need a locksmith to come and open or break a jammed lock or to fit a new lock (after a burglary, say), you can get the names of reliable firms in your area from the Master Locksmiths Association at 63 Surbiton Road, Kingston upon Thames, Surrey KT1 2HG.

assistance from public authorities

The services available to the public are not uniform thoughout the country and are better in some areas than in others. For elderly, infirm, handicapped people or those in straitened financial circumstances, there are in some places organisations prepared to give practical help as well as advice. Enquire at the local citizens advice bureau, local council for voluntary service or similar; some organisations have a panel of retired people with specialist skills, who volunteer to do minor jobs for pensioners and similar deserving cases.

electricity board

The electricity board will do a visual inspection of the house wiring free and will advise you whether your wiring system is in need of renewal. They have to attend to any fault affecting the meter, the external supply cable and its main fuse. Electricity boards also act as electrical contractors on a commercial basis (and are on the NICEIC approved roll).

Electricity boards run a 24-hour emergency service for breakdowns in the main supply and provide out-of-hours services for essential installation and appliance repairs. (The charge for this service is higher for calls at night.)

emergency services

A '999' telephone call is free, and no coins are needed from a public telephone. A '999' call is answered by the operator asking 'What service is required?'. Think which need is the more immediate – ambulance (in the case of injury or illness), fire, or police (in the case of burglary or other incident involving crime). You do not have to confine your request to only one; keep calm and the operator will help you to sort out priorities.

The fire brigade, apart from responding to a '999' call to deal with an outbreak of fire, will also come and help if a person is trapped or stuck – for example, in a lift. In a case of flooding, they can be asked to come to pump out basement premises.

gas region

The entry in the local telephone directory for emergency calls is under 'gas', not under the name of the local gas region, and a number is given to ring for urgent calls for gas escapes (a service man will come within an hour).

All leaks from appliances or an unaccounted-for smell of gas should be reported without delay to the gas region's emergency service. Someone will come to render the premises and supply safe. Checking a suspected escape, and simple repairs for this, will usually be free because the first 30 minutes of work are not charged for, including parts and materials up to the value of (at present) £1. If the service man attaches a warning label to an appliance stating that it must not be used, do not remove or disregard this label.

local authority
The names of the departments and the titles of the officers dealing with the various functions of a local authority are not standardised; you may need to start by tracking down the appropriate individual in your area. Most local authorities have an information telephone number or counter; also, the citizens advice bureau or a civic information centre will find out for you.

Infestation by pests, rats, mice, insects, damp and mildew and pollution by smells, noise and vibration usually come within the province of the environmental health office. Sewers and trees are generally dealt with by the engineer's or surveyor's department; in some authorities, the parks and gardens or recreation personnel may be responsible for trees.

telephone
If you are having difficulty obtaining connections or in receiving calls or the equipment or wires get damaged, notify the operator (use someone else's telephone, if necessary). Make clear what the problem is and arrange for access to your premises if this is necessary. If you get interference or unwanted calls (such as indecent communications) make a note of the time and circumstances and inform the operator who will put you in touch with the appropriate supervisor.

the water undertaking
The water undertaking (authority, company, council) is responsible for the maintenance of public sewers and if you live in a house where the drains from several premises connect to each other before joining

the public sewer, they may unblock the common part if this has become blocked. The service is usually free. However, a house owner is legally liable for the clearance of any obstruction and for maintenance of his drains right up to the point where the drain reaches the public sewer in the middle of the public highway.

The water undertaking (under 'w' in the telephone directory) will deal with leaks in the mains and will attend, mostly free of charge, to leaking cold water taps which are fed from the rising main. Otherwise, faults within your premises are your problem, although some authorities, for a charge, will attend to secondary taps (such as hot water) and ball valves. They also have lists of qualified plumbers who may be able to turn out for your job. The emergency service may also be able to send help if, for example, at weekends or holiday periods, you cannot find a plumber able to come to your rescue reasonably promptly.

The local authority, acting as agents for the water undertaking, runs an emergency service to clear obstructed public sewers and may also do so for private drains. Contact the engineer's department or environmental health department of the local authority if you cannot clear an obstruction in an outside drain. Whether you will be charged for this service depends on the local authority's criteria for what is a private drain (charged for) and when it turns into a public sewer (no charge). This may depend on the age of the installation and/or whether it is a drain that is shared with neighbouring properties. Many authorities have an emergency telephone number (listed in the telephone directory) for calls outside office hours.

Simple tools

It is unlikely that your bare fingers will be able to cope with more than a very few emergencies. So, assemble a standby tool kit and keep it handy, but not within the reach of small children. The object of this tool kit is to have a selection of essential items kept together and available for emergency use, rather than to be able to deal with every craft and d-i-y job around the house. Make – and keep – a resolution not to allow the tools to be used and abused for general odd-jobbing or to get dispersed, so that they will be there when urgently required, and in good order and condition.

Buying cheap tools may be a false economy. Do not be tempted to invest in combination multi-purpose do-everything miracle gadgets. If the novelty appeals to you and you do buy one, do not treat it as a substitute for a traditional implement or rely on it for serious work. Similarly, ready-collected bargain-priced sets of 'one of everything' are not recommended. The quality of some can be indifferent.

The basics include:

Pliers
What are generally referred to as 'combination' pliers will give a variety of actions – holding, turning, gripping to help pull or push things and cutting. Some pliers have insulating handles. However, this should not lull you into believing that the insulation will give you immunity from electric shock if the pliers are used to ferret about among live wires – it will not.

A second pair of pliers should have a long thin nose to be used for finer work and to reach into confined spaces. Again, it is an advantage, but not a 100 per cent safeguard, to get a pair with insulating handles.

When choosing pliers, bear in mind that the extent to which they will open depends not only on the hinge but also on how your hand will span the handles. So, if possible, try them for feel and how well you can hold them when there is something between their jaws. Pliers which look like a bandy-legged cowboy standing with his feet apart are no good for small fists but, at the other extreme, those with their heels tight together when closed might give the fleshy parts of your hand nasty nips when used for cutting. When you have found the pliers which suit you, make a test by holding them up against the light with their jaws closed: if you can see a gap or daylight coming through where the surfaces should meet, they have not been properly finished. Choose another pair without this fault.

For electrical work, you should have a pair of wire cutters and, unless you are adept at getting the insulating covering off wires without actually cutting into them, you will need a pair of wire strippers, too.

Screwdrivers
Generally, the larger the blade, the thicker the tip – which has to fit the slot of the screw. You will need (at least) three screwdrivers to use for the different sizes of slot in screw heads: one with a 4 to 6-inch blade, an 8-inch blade and a small 3-inch blade. The ratchet type can be set to lock in the direction of the drive and to freewheel in the recovery direction so that you do not need to release your grip on the handle. This is a time-saving refinement where a lot of work is intended, but a simple old-fashioned screwdriver with a good bulbous handle will be adequate for an emergency kit.

In addition, for electrical work, a screwdriver with a neon bulb inside the handle which will light up in contact with electricity could be useful.

A special type of screwdriver is needed for Phillips and Pozidriv screws which have '×' slots in their heads.

Hammers
There are so many varieties in shapes and sizes of hammer that making a choice is more a matter of elimination than picking one for its attributes.

Claw-headed Warrington or cross-pein   Ball-pein

A curved, claw-headed hammer combines several useful functions – for hitting, pulling and parting things. Hammers are graded by the weight of the head from 4 up to 24 oz. The 16 oz size would be heavy enough for most purposes.

To find out if the weight is suitable for you, hold the hammer at the end of the shaft, and give it several good positive swings. If this puts stress on your grip, wrist or forearm, choose a size lighter. In use, you will do better with a tool that you can wield conveniently and with confidence than one too heavy for you to control easily.

The 'V' in the claw head should be narrow and come well down (to give maximum leverage), tapered to a fine nick (to cater for small-headed pins). Since this tool is to be used for leverage, it needs a strong handle; traditionally, the handle is made of wood: straight-grained hickory, which has a bit of give and spring in it, or ash. The handle should be smooth in the hand (too open a grain can make for splinters).

For small nails and tacks, for getting at small spaces and for glazing jobs, a lighter hammer is needed – about half the weight of your claw-headed one – say, 8 oz or 6 oz or even 4 oz. A ball-pein hammer (with a rounded dome at one end of the head) would do, but a more useful style would be the Warrington or cross-pein. The narrow end of this is for getting into corners and hitting between finger and thumb when starting off small nails and pins. These hammers are not intended to be used for leverage, so the handles are slender; ash is quite satisfactory.

Spanners
To undo and get at anything that is held together by nuts and bolts, you will need a spanner. Spanners come with fixed or adjustable jaws.

For a fixed-jaw spanner, you have to have the right size to fit the nut.

An open-ended spanner fits on to nuts from the side; most open-ended spanners have jaws at both ends, each for a different size of nut. A ring spanner goes right round the nut. A combination spanner has a ring on one end and an open jaw at the other end.

Combination spanner

Most adjustable spanners are open-ended; one of the jaws can be moved closer and farther away from the other by a thumb wheel. If you have the correct size of spanner, use it in preference to an adjustable one because there will be less chance of spoiling the nut or bolt concerned.

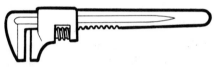

Adjustable spanner

The spanners called slip-joint pliers are slim, useful for getting into confined spaces.

Slip-joint pliers

For plumbing jobs, you may need a wrench, such as a stillson-type wrench with serrated movable jaws. You may need to use two, one for gripping, one for turning.

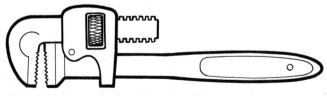

Stillson wrench

Knife and saw

Apart from tools for hitting, holding and turning things, you may need something for cutting. Any sharp fixed-blade knife which you find comfortable to use can be made to serve (but not a kitchen cast-off, which has probably had its day).

Useful would be one of the replaceable-blade knives, marketed under the generic name of trimming knives, in which a short length of blade slots into a handle held together by a screw. But a report in *Handyman Which?* November 1977 on trimming knives warns: 'A trimming knife has a sharp pointed blade and you can cut yourself while carrying it or picking it up. These injuries can be avoided if the blade is retracted out of harm's way or if a blade guard is in place. A blunt blade can be dangerous, so can an uncomfortable handle, and the angle at which you hold the blade to the work may be critical.'

Trimming knife

A 'junior' hacksaw (or a short hacksaw blade in a pad-saw handle) can be useful for cutting through metal. Opt for a fine rather than a coarse toothed blade for standby use – say, 18 or 24 tpi (number of teeth per inch of blade).

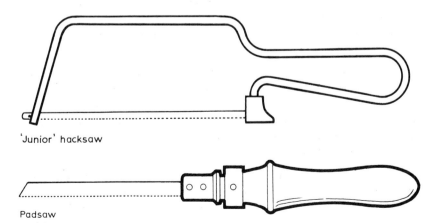

'Junior' hacksaw

Padsaw

File and chisel

A file could be useful, too. Files are graded according to the degree of roughness imparted by the size and spacing of the 'teeth'. The sequence runs: dead smooth, smooth, second-cut, bastard and rough. Second-cut will suit for your emergency kit; if you have to accept an alternative, opt for smooth in preference to the others. A 6-inch file should be quite big enough. Get one with a handle. Files are brittle and will not bend, so a file should not be used for levering, prising or chiselling.

A wood-working chisel may be worth having. The broader the chisel, the more power need to move it, but if you have too narrow a blade, you may find it is difficult to work with sufficient delicacy to avoid digging it in. A half-inch size is a useful one. Keep the chisel end in a sheath or embedded in an old cork, as a protection when not in use.

keeping your tools

Tools, if they are to be efficient, should be kept clean, dry and tidy, and cutting tools sharp. You could keep your tools in a cardboard box, but, if they are bunched together, you would have to scrabble amongst them to find the one you want. This is damaging to the tools in wear and tear, and is potentially dangerous for your hands – and a poor start to any emergency job. One of the metal haystack type of tool boxes, with two or three decks of trays, is a professional way of holding a collection of tools and has the advantage of allowing them to be kept in a segregated order. But it is somewhat expensive, perhaps, for only occasional use, and takes up a good deal of space. An inexpensive, plastic tool box would be quite adequate for an emergency kit, or even a lined biscuit tin.

If you can do a little sewing, or can persuade someone to do it for you, a compact tool roll can be made at very little cost. The unworn part of a discarded sheet or a piece of curtaining (which could look quite colourful) or a piece of hessian will serve. You need a piece about a yard or a metre wide, and the same or a bit more in length. Cut out a shape as shown in the sketch.

Hem it all round. If your material happens to have a selvedged edge, try to arrange this to come along the line G-H. Collect your tools and lay them out fairly close together side by side along, but at right angles

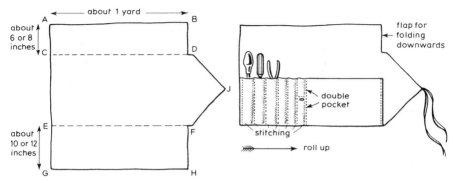

to, line E-F, lining them up like soldiers on parade with the tallest and thinnest on the left, graduated down to the shortest and fattest on the right. This should start you off with the big screwdriver on the left, making a good straight spine as a core to the roll.

Fold the flap E-F-G-H up over the tools and then pin in between the tools, not too tightly (or put tacking threads in), to make individually tailored tube-like pockets. Remove the tools and firmly sew down between the pockets. Some of the smaller items – say, small screwdrivers – may not need a pocket each and can go two to a pocket, one on top of the other. All this having been done, put your tools into their pockets in the same order as before, fold flap A-B-C-D over the tools, then roll up tightly from left to right, wrap the tab D-J-F around last and secure the whole with the tape or string fastening sewn on at J. This tool roll will leave space for future additions to the kit but do not sew up any more pockets at this stage: wait to see what items come into your possession and then make compartments to fit.

extras

Build up a cache of things likely to be useful in an emergency as a companion to your tool kit. Include a small magnet, handy for collecting spilt nails or pins or for recovering nuts, bolts and washers which have fallen into the recesses of appliances. A magnet will also save your finger ends by holding small nails or screws so that you can get them started with a hammer or screwdriver.

A roll of insulating tape (say, about ¾-inch wide) will come in useful. The type of insulating tape that is covered on both sides with a sticky black insulator is rather dirty to work with, but is pliable, and can be peeled off again if necessary. The tape with only one side coated comes in different colours and can be used for identifying which wire goes where when you dismantle any electrical equipment. Neither kind should be relied upon as being waterproof nor used as permanent insulation for any electrical part, wire or terminal. For electrical work, even for emergency use, the tape should be an adhesive tape complying with BS 3924.

Waterproof sealing tape, sold in hardware shops as p.t.f.e. (polytetrafluoroethylene) tape, or dry joint sealer, is a useful standby for sealing leaking pipes.

Sandpaper or emery paper or emery cloth of various grades may sometimes be needed, or a pad of fine gauge dry steel wool (store it in a dry place).

A can of penetrating oil, as an aerosol or with a dropper, is for lubricating, and for loosening rusty hinges or joints.

One or two aluminium foil milk bottle tops (thoroughly washed and dried, otherwise they will soon smell abominably) can come in handy for re-seating self-tapping screws that get loose in such appliances as washing machine, refrigerator, dishwasher.

Collect a selection of screws, nails, nuts, and bolts and washers (including any found around the house when cleaning – sooner or later it may come to light what it was they fell off). Keep them in a glass jar or clear plastic box.

In most houses, 3 and 13 amp cartridge fuses will be needed for plugs.

Other useful items include a rule or tape measure, a pencil or fibre tip pen for making marks, a clean dry rag or cloth, some string, scissors.

Two or three of the individually sealed-in dressing plasters will save you having to dash for the medical first-aid box if you happen to give yourself a nick. A small jar or tube of barrier cream to put on before tackling anything which looks like being a dirty or wet job will protect your hands. For cleaning up afterwards, a tin of all-purpose gel will help to remove grime, oil and so on from hands and clothing.

Some items come with special tools purpose-made for them. Take care of these, use them when needed in preference to any other general purpose tool, and do not let them get absorbed into the odd-job tool collection, to be used indiscriminately.

for electrical work
It may be useful to separate the items needed for an electrical emergency and to keep them near the main fuses:

a card of fuse wire of different ratings: 5, 15 and 30 amp; maybe 10 amp as well (or the appropriate cartridge fuses)
a screwdriver (the small neon-handle one)
roll of insulating tape
wire cutters/strippers (or a pair of small sharp pointed scissors)
a torch (one with a metal body can be used for testing cartridge fuses)
a multimeter.

A multimeter can be used for testing a faulty appliance or connection. Multimeters are available from about £8 – the more expensive the meter, the more complex and the more jobs can be done with it. You can use a simple multimeter, without needing much technical knowhow, to measure ohms as a continuity check for fuses and flexes, and, with care and experience, to check on the presence or absence of mains voltage. The instructions with the meter explain how to carry out the tests. Always follow them carefully.

Electrical emergencies

definitions of some electrical terms

conductor–any metal which conducts electricity: for example, the copper wires of a cable or flexible cord

insulation–non-conducting material used to cover conductor, to prevent contact

core (of a cable or flexible cord)–a conductor and its insulation, but not including any outer covering

cable–semi-rigid assembly of one or more cores used for fixed wiring in house

flexible cord (flex or lead)–flexible assembly of two or more cores, for connecting portable appliances and lamps to their plugs

sheath–insulating outer cover on cable or flexible cord to provide protection against mechanical damage

circuit–a complete metallic path permitting the flow of an electric current from its source to an appliance and back to the source

continuity–a continuous path of current between two points in a circuit

line conductor–outward conductor of a circuit, colloquially referred to as the 'live' conductor

phase conductor–recently introduced term for line conductor

neutral conductor–return conductor of a circuit (NB: both the phase and neutral conductors are live conductors)

colour coding–identifying colour of the cores in cables and flexible cords

for flexible cords: brown = line or phase ('live')
blue = neutral
green/yellow = earth

for flexible cords sold before July 1970:
red = line or phase ('live')
black = neutral
green = earth

for house wiring cables: red = line or phase ('live')
black = neutral
none, or green/yellow = earth

terminal–metallic device for connecting a conductor to a plug or to an appliance or to a socket; usually a screw or nut holding wires in place

fuse–deliberately weak link in a circuit intended to melt or 'blow' at a definite level of overcurrent so as to break the circuit and interrupt the current

short circuit–incorrect contact between live (phase and neutral) conductors, usually caused by failure of insulation, resulting in a surge of current

earth fault–fault similar to a short circuit, but due to incorrect contact between a live conductor and earth

earthing ⏚ –safety measure to ensure that in the event of an earth fault, current flows through the third (earth) conductor in a flex or cable sufficient to operate a shock-protective device, such as a fuse

double insulation ⊡ –method of protection against electric shock by enhanced insulation instead of earthing of exposed metallic parts (NB: double insulated appliances must not be earthed)

volt **(V)**–unit of electrical force or pressure needed to cause an electric current to flow in a circuit

ampere **(A)**–unit of electric current (rate of flow of electricity); the marking on a fuse or plug denotes the nominal current that it is designed to carry

watt **(W)**–unit of electric power used by a lamp or appliance

kilowatt **(kW)**–1000 watts

ohm **(Ω)**–unit of electrical resistance ($\Omega \times A = V$)

house wiring

In older houses with the wiring system known as radial, the sockets take round two-pin or three-pin plugs, for 2 or 5 or 15 amp appliances. There is a separate fuse on the main fuse board for each 15A power point as well as for the lighting circuits. Such a system usually has a number of fuse boxes due to additions in the course of the years.

From the early 1950's onwards, new wiring in houses has been of the ring circuit type. Ring circuits have only one size of socket outlet, with three rectangular holes – for flat 'square-pin' plugs. The same size of plug is used whether for a table lamp, heater, iron, refrigerator or any other appliance. The plug is designed to have a cartridge fuse in it and will not work without one. The fuse rating should match the appliance. Each ring circuit has a 30A fuse at the main fuse board (nowadays called the consumer unit).

For any electrical appliance (including lights) to work, there must be a complete electrical circuit. The fuse is the weakest link in the circuit, designed to break when a fault occurs, in order to protect the wiring from overheating (and causing a fire). It is a thin piece of wire, the thickness of which depends on the amount of electricity the circuit is designed to carry.

With the normal current passing through it, a fuse does not overheat. But if the circuit is overloaded (for instance, because too many appliances have been connected to it) or a very heavy current of electricity passes through it (for instance, due to a short circuit), the fuse becomes very hot and melts or breaks. This automatically cuts off the electric current through that circuit.

The types of current-breaking devices at the consumer unit that may be used in domestic wiring are re-wirable fuses, cartridge fuses and miniature circuit breakers. The fuse holder (or fuse carrier) for a re-wirable fuse made of ceramic material is easily damaged or broken. Never re-use a broken fuse holder: replace it with a new one. A re-wirable fuse consists of a strand of tinned copper or aluminium wire in the fuse holder. This wire is of different thickness according to the amount of current that it is designed to carry, such as 5A, 10A, 15A, 20A and 30A. The amperage is marked on the fuse holder or on the lid of the fuse box.

In a cartridge fuse, the wire is contained in a small tube or cylinder which is sealed at each end with a metal cap and clips into the fuse holder. These devices cannot be repaired and if one fails, a new cartridge fuse of the appropriate rating has to be fitted. The rating is indicated on the holder in figures and by a colour coding: white for 5A, blue for 15A, yellow for 20A, red for 30A, green for 45A. The British Standard for these fuses is BS 1361.

As a general rule, circuits that feed the lights are unlikely to be fused at a value greater than 5A, normally with a different fuse for each floor in the house. Each ring circuit for a number of square-holed sockets has a 30A fuse in the fuse box. Electric cookers, storage heaters, water heaters and similar large electrical loads have their own circuits, each protected by a fuse of the appropriate rating.

re-wirable fuse
When a re-wirable fuse blows, you must switch off the main supply at the consumer unit before you attempt anything else.

If you have been prudent enough to identify which of your fuses protect which sockets and lights, you will be able to go straightaway to the appropriate one. Failing that, identification will have to be by trial and error, taking out each fuse carrier in turn until you find the culprit: a broken wire and possibly a scorch mark. (If you have not got the fuses marked, now is the time, while you are investigating, to label each of them – to save you time and trouble in future.)

First, you have to clear out the remains of the burnt wires from the fuse carrier and wipe off the scorch marks, and loosen the terminals on the carrier. Be sure to replace a burned-through fuse wire with one of the appropriate rating for the current it will have to take. Do not use anything other than the correct wire. Cut off an appropriate length (about 3 inches), allowing enough to wind round the screws. Thread the new piece of fuse wire into the carrier and fasten one end round one terminal in the direction in which the screw is tightened, and then wind the other end once round the other terminal anti-clockwise; screw the terminals up again. Allow a little slack in the fuse wire when fastening it to the second terminal so that it is not stretched or snapped when the screw is tightened. Cut off any protruding ends of wire. Make sure that the main switch is turned off before you replace the fuse carrier.

cartridge fuse

Cartridge fuse holders look much the same from the outside as the re-wirable type, but the old cartridge fuse can be unclipped and the new one inserted in a matter of seconds.

First of all, switch off the main supply. It is not possible to tell by just looking which fuse has gone. In a booklet, *Electricity for everyday living* published by the Electrical Association for Women, the following tip is given for finding out if a cartridge fuse is still working:

Take out the most likely fuse carrier, e.g. if the lights have gone out, remove one of the fuse carriers marked 5A (white). Unscrew the two portions, remove the cartridge fuse and check that the fuse is intact.

To do this use a torch with a metal case. Switch the torch on so that it lights up. Unscrew the bottom cap and place the cartridge fuse so that one of the metal ends touches the metal base of the battery and the other makes contact with the metal of the torch case. If the torch lights, the fuse is intact and can be replaced in the carrier. Continue checking the fuses in turn until the torch fails to light which will indicate that the fuse has blown and needs replacing. Place a new cartridge fuse of the correct size in the carrier, screw the two sections together and replace the fuse carrier. Close the box and then turn 'on' the main switch.

If a torch with a metal casing is not available, replace the fuse in the carrier with another fuse of the same rating, close the box and switch 'on' the main switch. If the faulty fuse has not been located, switch 'off' the main switch again and replace the cartridge fuse in another fuse carrier. Repeat until the faulty fuse has been found, remembering to switch 'off' the main switch each time before removing or replacing the fuse carrier, and to replace the blown cartridge fuse with one of the same rating.

if fuse blows again

Should the fuse blow yet again, do not, whatever you do, be tempted to replace it with a higher rated wire or fuse: the fuse may not blow quickly enough when there is a fault and would allow too large an amount of current to flow. This could allow the wires in the cable or in the flex to an appliance to overheat, and cause a fire.

If a fuse blows frequently, or the fuse carrier is found to be very hot to the touch, switch off all the appliances (ideally, disconnect them at the socket outlet) and recheck the temperature of the fuse holder. If it is still hot, there is probably a fault in the wiring of the house. If the fuse holder is no longer hot, either the fault is on an appliance or its flexible cord, or the circuit was overloaded (for instance, too many heaters plugged in at the same time).

Any fault that seems to be due to a failure in the house wiring should be investigated promptly by a qualified electrical contractor. A large proportion of the fires that occur in households originate in faulty electrical wiring.

circuit breakers

Nowadays in newer houses, miniature circuit breakers may be installed instead of main fuses on each ring circuit. A miniature circuit breaker (m.c.b.) is a device which opens automatically under conditions of overload and so breaks the electric circuit. An m.c.b. has to have the rating appropriate to the circuit on which it is installed.

Miniature circuit breakers give a visual indication of which circuit has a fault (but you then have to identify which outlet within the circuit has created the fault). Miniature circuit breakers do not have to be removed from the consumer unit. When they 'trip', the button on the face pops out or the switch goes into the 'off' position. Only when the fault has been cleared can the button be pressed in again, or the switch turned to the 'on' position and stay in or on.

In some country districts, with overhead wiring, a protective device called an earth leakage circuit breaker may have been installed, which should disconnect the main supply when a fault in any part of the installation or an appliance causes voltage along the earth line. When the trip operates, everything electrical in the house is put out of action. Earth leakage circuit breakers have a test button which should be pressed at regular intervals to make sure the circuit breaker is working properly.

total failure

If all the power and lights in the house fail, the explanation may be something simple, such as a power cut or interruption to the main electricity supply. If it is night time, look at the street lights or neighbours' houses to see whether any lights are on (but bear in mind in country districts nearby houses are not necessarily on the same main supply line). If there are no lights visible, it is likely that there is a general area failure. If the lights in other houses are on, the trouble most likely lies in the installation on your own premises.

If the installation in your house has an earth leakage circuit breaker, see if it has tripped. If it has, reset the trip and see what happens. If it trips again, locate where the trouble is.

The chances are that the trip has been set off by some fault in the earthing of an appliance. The way to check on this is to unplug the appliances and switch off the lights. Reset the breaker, then plug in and switch on appliances and lights one at a time: when the trip is set off again, it shows that the fault lies with whatever you have just switched on.

In a house without an earth leakage circuit breaker, no power or lights anywhere probably means that the main electricity supply has failed, or that the electricity board's fuse has blown. This fuse is sealed in, and must not be interfered with by you. The action to take is to telephone the electricity board (on the emergency number) so that someone can be sent to reinstate the supply.

an appliance fails to work

For an electrical appliance to work, it has to be connected to the live conductors in the wiring of a house, via the 'live' and neutral conductors in the flex leading to the appliance, so that the electric circuit is completed through the appliance when you switch on.

If an appliance fails to work, the cause is likely to be a blown fuse or a faulty connection somewhere, usually in the plug.

If there is a failure in the insulation, most of the current will take the path of lower resistance either to the other conductor (a short circuit), or to a metal part of the appliance and thence through the earth conductor. The ensuing surge of current to earth should blow the fuse, thereby cutting off the electricity.

The first thing to do is to disconnect the appliance. Examine the flex and the plug to see whether there is anything obviously wrong – for instance, damaged flex or loose connection.

You should look at the connections of the wires to the terminals in the plug and, where possible, in the appliance itself. Make sure that none of the wires has come loose from its terminal. If it has, refix it properly.

If it is a fused plug, one way of checking whether a cartridge fuse has blown is to take it out of the plug of the appliance which has failed and put it into an appliance (of similar rating) that is in working order. If it goes on working, the fuse is still good. Alternatively, check on a metal torch – or use a multimeter if you have one. Cartridge fuses sometimes fail for no apparent cause or die through old age.

If the fuse is dead, replace it in the plug with one of the correct rating, and try again. If the appliance still fails to work, you have to go on looking for the fault.

If the house wiring is the radial system with round pin plugs, the fuse is not in the plug: you will have to go to the fuse board, switch off, find the appropriate fuse, withdraw and check it. If it is blown, rewire with the correctly rated fuse wire.

An appliance may fail because the flex has cracked or broken, usually at a point where maximum movement takes place, near where it enters the appliance or the plug. (If you have a multimeter, you can use it to test each conductor for continuity. If this shows that the flex is faulty, you have to replace it.)

If a flex is worn, frayed or shows signs of other deterioration, it should be cut back beyond that point or replaced.

replacing flex

Flex is rated in amps according to the electrical current it can carry.

On the whole, 3A flex is suitable for lights, 6A for low rated appliances such as a vacuum cleaner, 10A for wattages between 1kW and 2kW (for example, a two-bar heater), 13A or 15A for more powerful appliances. Flex is also designated in square millimetres, namely: $0.5mm^2$ (3A), $0.75mm^2$ (6A), $1.0mm^2$ (10A), $1.25mm^2$ (13A), $1.5mm^2$ (15A).

For appliances taking a lot of current, such as an electric fire, the major consideration is that the wires within the flex shall be able to carry the current involved.

The higher the amperage, the more wires there are in the conductors and the thicker the flex. It does not matter using a flex of a higher rating than the appliance requires, but flex costs more the higher its rating. Also, it may not be possible to fit all the strands of a thick flex into small terminals – and you must never cut out strands of wire.

For an appliance that gets a lot of moving around, such as an iron, or a vacuum cleaner, you could save further wear and trouble by buying non-kink flex that will not get twisted up in use – it costs a little more, but is generally worth it.

An appliance that requires earthing must not be fitted with a 2-core flex.

To replace the flex, you must undo the casing of the appliance to get at the terminals inside. Do not attempt the dismantling of an electrical appliance unless you know that you are able to restore it properly.

When you do dismantle an electrical appliance to take out the old flex, do it if possible on a flat, plain surface, with the necessary tools to hand, and work systematically. As you take them off, study the location of the various items such as the cord grip (the clamp which helps to take the strain off the terminals). Arrange screws, washers etc in the order you take them off, so that you can reassemble them in the correct order.

Make a note of the colour coding and positioning of the conductors at their terminals before you dismantle the flex from the appliance so that you can connect the new flex correctly. Remember that the flex on an old appliance may have the old colour coding (red for live, black for neutral, green for earth).

The flexes running from ceiling roses to pendant lamp holders are affected by heat rising from the lamps below, and also subject to mechanical stress from the weight of the light fittings. Inspect these flexes whenever you change a bulb and get replaced any that show signs of becoming old, heat-stained or brittle. Heat-resisting flexes are available.

rewiring a plug

You must never connect a 3-core flex to a two-pin plug. It is essential that the wires in the flex go to the correct terminals in the plug. Connection of the earth wire to the live terminal would make the whole metal casing of the appliance live, and very dangerous: if you touched any metal part, you would get a shock, possibly lethal. Cross-connection of the live and neutral wires would mean that any switch on the appliance, although effective, would not cut off the current in the live conductor – also potentially dangerous: although the appliance is inactive, there is current still in it.

Most plugs have their terminals marked L, N, E. The L stands for line or live and the brown coloured conductor should be connected to it. N stands for neutral and the blue coloured conductor should be connected to it. E or ⏚ stands for earth and the green/yellow coloured conductor should be connected to it.

After undoing the screw or screws which hold the plug together, take off the lid section and hold the flex with the conductors over their correct terminals. Looking into the opened plug with the flex entry point at the bottom, the neutral (blue) wire has to be fitted to the terminal on the left, the live (brown) to the terminal on the right. In a fused flat pin plug, the clips for the cartridge fuse are at the live terminal. The earth terminal is the top one of the three, connecting to the large pin of the plug. In most plugs, the earth conductor needs to be longer than the other two in order to reach its terminal; also, allow for a little slack, so that if the flex were to get a sharp tug, the earth conductor will not be pulled off its terminal.

The outer covering of the flex should be stripped off to a point just inside the cord grip on the plug which is to hold the flex in position. Cut off each conductor about $\frac{3}{8}$ inch beyond the centre of the terminal to which it is to be connected. About half an inch of the insulation (less in a plug in which the bared wires have to go through a hole in the terminal) should be removed from the end of each conductor, leaving the insulation over the wires intact up to the terminal. The insulation can be removed with a sharp penknife, a pair of pliers or wire strippers. Be careful when stripping off the insulation not also to cut strands of wire. Twist the bared wires of each conductor into a smooth end. Loosen the cord grip (if it is a screw-up type) and pass the flex through or under it and tighten it so that it grips on the flex.

In some plugs, the terminals have a hole through which the wires have to be pushed and screwed down; you may need to double the end of the wires over for the screw to get a firm grip. In plugs with terminals

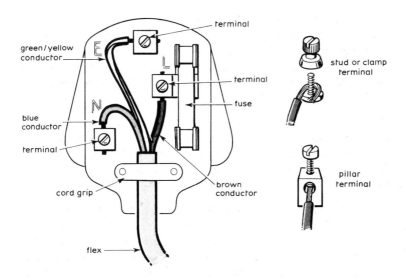

round which the wires have to be wrapped, bend the wires round the terminal in a clockwise direction so that, when you screw down the terminal, it draws the wires round it and secures them firmly. It is important that the screw is tightly down on the wires, particularly on the earth conductor. Be careful not to allow any whiskers to stick out: if all the strands of wire are not held by the terminal screw, the plug may overheat. Similarly, make sure that none of the coloured insulating sheath round the wire is trapped under the terminal screw – this would result in a poor connection, and also cause overheating.

For a fused plug, make sure that the fuse is of the right rating and is one marked BS 1362.

Make sure that the flex is held firmly in the cord grip, at the point where the flex enters the plug. The cord grip is there to take strain off the terminals. If the flex is held only by the terminals, a sharp tug on the flex might pull wires away from the terminal, so that bare ends are loose inside. At best, this would mean that the circuit is broken, and the appliance will not work. But if the ends of wire happen to touch, it will cause a short circuit. If a pull on the flex had also disconnected the earth conductor, there would be no protection from the earthing system.

If you are connecting a 2-core flex to a three-pin plug, use only the live and neutral terminals in the plug and ignore the earth terminal. You must connect the live conductor to the L terminal and the neutral to the N terminal. This is especially important if the appliance has a switch on it, to ensure that the current is switched off where it enters the appliance, not where it leaves it. Some 2-core flex is colour coded, too. If not, and the insulation of the two conductors is joined together like siamese twins and the insulation on one has a rib running along, it is to show that this conductor should be connected to the live terminal.

On a two-pin round plug, when you look into the opened plug, with flex entry point at the bottom, live is on the right of point of entry, neutral to the left.

common appliance faults

Always read the manufacturer's or supplier's brochures and instructions carefully before using any appliance the first few times, and take particular note of any warnings that are given. Do not assume it works like a previous model you may have used or seen in action.

If you are not sure what the instructions mean, go back to where you got the appliance and ask for an explanation or demonstration. Any reputable dealer would prefer you to do this rather than have a problem on his hands through your inadvertent misuse of what he has supplied.

Keep brochures and instruction booklets safely in a specific place. Put them into a plastic see-through bag or cover to keep them clean and visible. Now and again take time to refresh your memory by re-reading them to make sure that you have not fallen into bad habits of misusing an appliance.

Most manufacturers nowadays recommend that their appliances are sent back to the factory, or to one of their service agents, for repair. This may be a condition of the guarantee. Some manufacturers and retailers now offer a 5-year guarantee.

Many modern electrical devices are made not to be repairable; there may be nothing that can be done about an appliance that has gone wrong – except buy a new one. In some older appliances, parts are replaceable, such as elements in fires or toasters. Do not tackle any such job unless you are sure that you can see it through to a successful and safe conclusion.

When an appliance does not work, first check that it is plugged in firmly, switched on and correctly set and, where appropriate, that the thermostat is in order.

If you can find no fault on the appliance or the plug but it does not work when you plug in, check if the socket is at fault. Plug in some other appliance that you know is working. If it does not come on, the fault is probably in the wiring to the socket (and may have blown the main fuse at the consumer unit). A fault in the socket or the wiring is one for an experienced electrician to identify and put right.

–dismantling
Do not go poking around in any appliance while it is still plugged in. Not only can you do the appliance a mischief, you can injure (or kill) yourself. It is vital to disconnect the appliance from the mains. Do not just switch if off: unplug it.

If you attempt to dismantle an appliance, proceed methodically, making a note of the relative positioning of components as you go. Inspect parts carefully to see the order of their assembly and note particularly where the earth wire is attached to the metal casing. Be wary of various bits and pieces that could fly out under spring pressure.

washing machine
In the event of leaking or flooding, the first thing to do is to unplug the machine from the electricity supply (not just switching off the machine) and to turn off the water supply.

The leak or flooding may be caused by a loose hose; split hose; faulty pump; leaking drum; leaking front seal; faulty solenoid-operated tap; faulty water level sensor – or human error, such as putting in too much powder, putting in ordinary washing powder instead of low suds powder, or an obstruction causing a blocked outlet.

If you find a loose hose, tighten the connection to tap, spout or joint. If an outlet is blocked, clear it. To check if a hose is split or perished, bend the hose through a small radius to see if cracks can be opened up by doing so. In the case of an outlet hose, you may be able to see from dried marks on the machine (or the floor) where soapy water has been getting out. A hose can be replaced without too much expertise, but some are tricky to get to.

You ought to be able to see simply by looking if water is leaking out around the front seal, or if the water level in the drum is higher than normal. If the solenoid-operated tap, or its associated sensor unit, is not operating properly, the water will continue to go into the drum and you will see the water level rising long after it ought to have stopped. You will have to call in the repair man.

If the machine stops by itself in the middle of the washing cycle, the timer may have gone wrong. Check by switching to another part of the cycle: if the drum then revolves, the motor is still functioning so the timer is the likely offender, and you will need a new one.

A kinked hose will stop intake of water, possibly preventing the machine advancing, and a blocked pump will restrict pumping out, with similar results. Repositioning the hose is likely to remove the kink. Dealing with a pump should only be attempted by someone who knows how.

If the drum does not revolve, the cause may be wear in the drive motor (prime suspect: the carbon brushes – get them replaced) or a loose connection on the timer. If the drum itself does not revolve but the motor does, the cause may be a worn drive belt. Get the drive belt tightened or replaced.

Excessive vibration of a washing machine or spin drier is usually caused by bad loading of the machine rather than by the machine maulfunctioning. Switch off, open the door, rearrange the load, and start the machine again.

To get rid of the water in a machine that has stopped in mid-cycle, you will have to bail it out with a jug or saucepan. For a front loader, have a square washing up bowl or a metal waste paper bin ready to catch as much of the water as possible as you open up.

twin tub
If the paddle in a rotary-operated washer tangles and chews up the clothes, the cause may be too heavy a load or too little water. If an agitator-type washer stops, the cause may be that too heavy a load has locked the paddle or stalled the motor.

Non-starting in a twin tub is most likely due to insufficient water – it has to be well up to and a shade over the line marked in the tub, the level where the sensor (thermostat) is which triggers off the agitator. If the water is not up to this line, however hot it gets, it will not set off the sensor.

Generally, whenever a paddle or agitator jams, it may just be that some small item has got caught up – search and dislodge. The same applies to a blockage of water: something (accumulated fluff or small item) may be lying over the intake to the circulating pump at the bottom of the tub under the paddle: clean or clear it.

refrigerator, freezer

Refrigerators are among the most reliable of motor-driven electrical appliances. They can become less efficient but are unlikely to cause an emergency situation.

If there is a power cut or the supply has been switched off, treat this as an unorthodox defrost: leave the refrigerator door open and put in a tray to catch the melting ice.

For a freezer, however, do not open the door or lid. The food is unlikely to be harmed for some hours. Even when the power has been restored, keep the freezer closed for at least an hour. If the disconnection was for longer than, say, nine hours, check the condition of the contents – do not refreeze anything that has started to thaw but move it to the ordinary refrigerator, ready to eat soon. If in doubt, do not eat. (You may be able to reclaim the cost if insured.)

iron

The flex on an electric iron is subject to wear, and to strain if, for instance, someone trips over it or it is dropped awkwardly, and also if you persistently iron too far away from the socket.

A common fault is the flex fraying at a point where it runs over and rubs against the edge of the ironing board or table. If fraying gets so bad that the insulation round the conductors is eroded, this is potentially lethal. There are various flex-protecting devices and flex holders to keep the flex from rubbing against the table or board.

Renew the flex as soon as fraying becomes apparent. You have to unscrew or undo part of the iron to get at the terminals; this may be fiddly on some irons. Remember to notice the positions and order of things as you undo them, so that you can put them back correctly. It is particularly important that the cord grip is tightly secured. Use three-core non-kink flex appropriate to the wattage of the iron.

In time, the element itself may burn out. An element may be replaceable but the iron has to be dismantled, and the thermostat setting checked afterwards. But on many irons the element is integral with the sole plate, which would have to be replaced as well, probably making it an uneconomic repair.

Do not fill (or empty) a steam iron while it is plugged in: switch off, unplug, then fill.

If steam comes from a (steam) iron but not through the sole plate, you may scorch what you are ironing. The cause is probably clogged-up vents or nozzle. Unplug the iron. When cool, probe the nozzle with the end of a piece of fine fuse wires; the perforations in the sole plate may be cleared with a needle. A special descaling fluid is available for use in a steam iron.

Most irons have an adjustable thermostat which turns the current on and off to keep the iron at a temperature around that set on the termostat dial. When the iron is first switched on, it takes some time for the heat to travel from the element to the thermostat and the iron therefore overshoots the chosen temperature before it settles down, usually within five minutes. The period for the temperature to stabilise depends on the design of the iron and its loading: it can be as long as eight minutes. For this reason, the instructions for some irons recommend that you should not use the iron for anything up to 10 minutes after first switching on.

When an iron gets either too hot or not hot enough, it is probably because the thermostat has gone wrong and drifted off its original settings.

You can tell whether the thermostat is functioning at all by moving the control dial and listening for the click that it should make. (If the indicator light fails to come on, it may just be that its bulb has gone.) If you hear no click at all, the thermostat most likely is jammed, and you will need to get a new one, properly calibrated.

thermostats

A thermostat is a device controlling the flow of current to an appliance by opening or closing the electrical circuit when a chosen temperature is reached. It can be made to operate between certain temperature limits or at a fixed temperature.

The function of one type of fixed thermostat is to act as a safety cut-out, and protect the appliance from getting overheated. They are set to operate in good time, and therefore have a wide tolerance; they rarely fail.

A wide tolerance is not acceptable for the variable type of thermostat, such as is in an iron, which has to operate within fairly fine limits if the fabric is not to be scorched. Recalibrating a thermostat should be done by an electrical retailer or contractor with specialised equipment.

A few appliances have a fixed thermostat cut-out as a back-up to the variable sort, as a safety feature.

heating appliances

Hairdriers and fan heaters both have a heating element, with a fan to propel air through it and a sensor for the thermostat in the air flow.

The manufacturers' instructions normally warn against restricting the air supply. If the air inlet to the appliance is obstructed, the temperature will rise excessively and trip the thermostatic cut-out. Unplug and let the appliance cool down, then clear the obstruction.

If only cold air is being emitted, either the heater element or the heat control switch has failed. These components could be replaced by a handy-person – or take the appliance to an electrical repairer.

If the fan slows down or stops, the cut-out should operate to stop the element from overheating. The slowing down may well have a mechanical cause – encrustations of dirt, or maybe dry motor bearings. Unplug, dismantle and clean thoroughly. Spin the fan with your finger: if it is stiff to turn, put a single drop of fine machine oil on each bearing. But sometimes when the casing is removed, it is difficult to reassemble – bits tend to spring out and you would need to know how to fit them back together.

If the casing of a hairdrier gets cracked or broken, there is the danger that moisture from your hands may find its way in through the crack on to a live part, conducting electricity from that part to you and giving you at best a lively tickle, but possibly a severe or even fatal shock. Take no chances: if you cannot get the crack in the casing permanently sealed, or if any bits have broken off, throw it away.

In a radiant electric fire, failure to heat up may be due to broken element wire (replace with a new element of the same size and rating), a loose element mounting (tighten), a faulty switch (get it replaced), a loose connection (check whether a pull on the flex has broken one of the wires or one of the terminals has become loose and the wires moved).

Unplug before attempting an investigation or repair.

electric blanket
A faulty electric blanket is emphatically not a do-it-yourself repair job. Even the flex is not usually replaceable because, as a precaution against pulling out, it is often bonded directly into the blanket.

If the fault is caused by a broken element or a non-functioning thermostat, send the blanket back to the manufacturer to be repaired; do not attempt to do it yourself.

It could be cheaper in the long run – what with the cost of postage and repair charges – to cut your losses and buy a new blanket (this will also solve the problem more quickly).

Check the blanket regularly for frayed parts, loose connections, signs of wear, crossed or tangled element wires (usually you can see these by holding the blanket up to a strong light). Examine the flex for signs of deterioration.

Because an electric blanket is a potential fire hazard, it is important always to follow the manufacturer's instructions about using, storing and servicing.

vacuum cleaner
If a cylinder vacuum cleaner is running badly, it may be because the carbon 'brushes' in the motor are worn and need renewing. Unplug

the cleaner, open the casing to get to the brushes. (These are two small pieces of carbon which press, one on each side, on a set of copper segments.) On some designs, you have to remove the motor from the cylinder to do this; others merely need the front casing taken off. When you take the brushes out, be sure to notice how they fit so that you can replace them the same way round. You must get the brushes intended for that particular machine. When you have installed new brushes, check that the motor is free to turn, before enclosing it again.

The upright type of vacuum cleaner has more moving parts, usually driven by the motor via what looks like an outsize rubber band. If the motor whirrs, but the machine does not beat, sweep or clean efficiently, the odds are that the drive belt has stretched, slipped off or broken. Unplug, turn the machine upside down to look. Replacing a drive belt is a fiddly job but within the competence of a handy-person.

A suddenly stalled motor or an unusual noise in an upright vacuum cleaner is sometimes caused by something metallic or hard having been picked up – a hairpin, nail, stone or the like – which jams the fan blades against the casing. Unplug, and then rock the spindle from which the driving belt takes its motion, to and fro with a rotary movement, starting with an anti-clockwise turn. You may need pliers to do this, in which case wrap something around the spindle first to avoid making scratches which could cause wear on the belt. One or two wiggles should release the obstruction. It is preferable to try to extract it by shaking it out forwards (whence it went in), rather than endeavouring to get it to go onwards through the bag.

In a cylinder cleaner, the sucking tube may get blocked – perhaps by crumpled paper, such as a sweet wrapper, which unfolds on its way up the tube. The hose can usually be cleared by disconnecting it from the 'suck' end and replacing it on the 'blow' end of the cleaner. Lay it flat and as straight as possible before switching on.

Avoid putting undue strain on the flex and terminals by stretching the flex too far when using the cleaner. Do not pull out the plug by pulling on the flex. Inspect the flex from time to time to see that the insulation has not worn, particularly at the entry point to the cleaner.

kitchen appliances

In a kitchen there is usually a number of portable electrical appliances each with a flex which could accidentally be damaged by a heat source or cutting edge. Do not let a flex or plug get wet or touch a hot surface; try not to have long trailing flexes. And remember to switch off at the socket before taking out the plug.

Should any flex get damaged in any way or start to fray, do not be tempted just to wrap a piece of insulating tape around the worn or damaged part (except as a short-term temporary emergency measure): replace the flex.

With wet hands, there is a grave danger of electric shock. Do not go on using any faulty appliance once you know, or suspect, it is faulty.

Never immerse any electric appliance in water. Should this happen inadvertently, do not use it again until it has thoroughly dried out. Give it ample time to do this: it may take weeks. It would need only a vapour of moisture or a film of dampness clinging to the components inside to cause an electrical short circuit, with its accompanying blown fuse, when the current is switched on.

To be on the safe side, do not fill the kettle while it is connected, even if it is switched off. When the kettle is not in use, unplug it from the wall socket so that if it is switched on by mistake, it does not activate the connector which may be plugged into an empty kettle or lying loose, perhaps near water. Keep the connector away from the sink in case contact with water causes a shock.

Quite apart from any device the kettle may have to switch off when the water is boiling, there will be a thermal cut-out device to disconnect the electric current if the kettle is allowed to boil dry or is used with insufficient water. One type resets itself when the element has cooled down, or may have to be reset by pressing a small peg or button inside the connector socket. With the type that ejects the connector, the ejecting pin needs to be pushed back again with some considerable force (use, for example, the handle of a wooden spoon) before the connector will fit again into the kettle.

On an electric cooker with radiant rings, if you notice that a ring is glowing unusually brightly or has one over-bright spot on it, this shows that the element is failing and you should get a new one fitted.

electric appliance*	in wattage range	rating of fuse(amps) to use	
		at fuse box with round pin plug	in flat pin plug†
battery charger	50W	5	3
blanket	60–150W	5	3
can opener	60W	5	3
coffee grinder	100W	5	3
coffee maker/percolator	up to 750W	5	3
	750W–1kW	5	13
cooker, portable	3kW	15	13
dishwasher	up to 3kW	15	13
drill	up to 500W	5	3/13‡
food mixer	100–450W	5	3
food processor	up to 750W	5	13
freezer	300W	5	3/13‡
frying pan/fryer	750W–1½kW	15	13
hairdrier	up to 720W	5	3
	over 1kW	15	13
hair rollers	450–700W	5	3
heaters: convector	1–3kW	15	13
fan	2–3kW	15	13
oil-filled	up to 500W	5	3
	1–3kW	15	13
radiant	1–3kW	15	13
hot plate/trolley	up to 750W	5	13
iron	750W–1250W	5/15	13
ironing machine	1½kW	15	13
kettle	750W–1kW	5	13
	1–3kW	15	13
lamps, standard and table	100W	5	3
mains radio	50W	5	3

electric appliance*	in wattage range	rating of fuse(amps) to use at fuse box with round pin plug	in flat pin plug†
microwave oven	1½–2kW	15	13
power tool	up to 500W	5	3/13‡
record/cassette player	75W	5	3
refrigerator	about 100W	5	3/13‡
rotisserie	2kW	15	13
sewing machine	100W	5	3
slide projector	200W	5	3
slow-cooking pot	50–150W	5	3
spin drier	about 300W	5	3/13‡
TV set	up to 350W	5	3/13‡
small portable	up to 50W	5	3
toaster	up to 750W	5	3
	750–1600W	15	13
tumble drier	2–3kW	15	13
vacuum cleaner	up to 750W	5	3/13‡
	750W–1kW	15	13
washing machine	2½–3kW	15	13
waste disposer	up to 500W	5	3/13‡

* **basic rule**
with round pin plug: for appliance up to 1000W = 5A
over 1000W = 15A
in flat pin plug: for appliance up to 720W = 3A
over 720W = 13A

† usually supplied with 13A fuse within; if for low-rated appliance, fuse must be changed to 3A
colour code for cartridge fuses: red = 3A, brown = 13A

‡ the higher fuse rating needed for extra current when starting up

avoiding electrical emergencies

Make sure that the fuse in a fused plug is of the correct rating. Never use a fuse of a rating higher than the current demand of the appliance. For example, if you use a 13A fuse with a low wattage appliance, it may not blow in time to protect an overloaded flex.

If any plug, socket, flex, switch or part of an appliance is getting noticeably hot, this can be an indication that something is wrong. A plug with a 13-amp fuse in it gets quite warm when carrying a heavy load such as a three-bar (3kW) heater. But a plug should never feel unpleasantly hot to the touch and the flex should never feel more than slightly warm. If there is a smell of hot rubber or plastic, the insulation covering the wires has started to overheat. Switch off and disconnect and try to trace the trouble.

If a switch starts working erratically or gets hot, it shows that the spring or contacts are worn. Get the switch replaced.

Adaptors are useful to connect two appliances to one socket but the total wattage taken by the two appliances must not exceed the rating of the socket into which the adaptor is plugged. A 13A socket outlet can supply up to 3000 watts (3kW). If you exceed this figure, the fuse may blow or both the socket and the adaptor get very hot and be damaged and could eventually cause a fire. If you use an adaptor, make sure that it is a fused one so that its fuse protects the wiring.

If you need to use adaptors frequently, it would be better to have some more socket outlets installed.

You can often tell when a connection in a plug is loose by shaking it: if you hear things rattling around – open it, check and tighten the terminal screws.

You should never remove a plug from its socket by pulling on the flex: this causes strain on the cord grip and may loosen wires from their terminal. On a switched socket, always switch off before removing the plug or putting it in.

The insulation of flexes can get brittle. To check, disconnect the appliance, twist the flex round your finger, listen for crackling, and then inspect the covering for cracking. In an extreme case, the insulation will fall straight off. The flex will need to be replaced – not just repaired with insulating tape.

check list
If appliance does not work
- check everything is switched on

if it still does not work
- check whether correctly fitted and set

if it still does not work
- check appliance in another socket where another appliance works

if it still does not work
- check connections to terminals in plug

if it still does not work
- change fuse (if in plug)

if it still does not work
- check main circuit fuse

if it still does not work
- check connections to terminals inside appliance

if it still does not work
- get electrician to look at it.

If it is something you can carry, take it for repair to a qualified electrical contractor. If you have to call a service engineer or repair man to come to you, give full details of the make and model and other identifying number of the appliance. You may find these in the instruction book and on the rating plate. Describe what has happened or gone wrong as concisely and accurately as possible. Give your address, also accurately: you may have to pay for time spent travelling to you. Also, there may be a minimum or a call-out charge. Ask on what basis you will be charged.

Leaks and blockages

Damp patches on the ceiling can be due to a leak in a water pipe, or at the cold water cistern in the loft, perhaps because of a blocked overflow pipe or a worn washer.

If the ceiling is beginning to bulge, put buckets and bowls underneath and spike a couple of holes in the lowest part of the bulge to release the water, otherwise the whole ceiling may collapse. If there is any possibility of water getting near to or running along electric wiring, disconnect the circuit at the fuse board.

In old houses that have lead plumbing, pin holes can occur at any point along the length. You can reduce a leak in a lead pipe by very gently tapping all around it with a rounded end of a ball pein hammer. Hold the hammer at about 45° to the pipe, tap in a circle around the hole, gradually decreasing the circle size. Since lead is a very malleable metal, this gentle tapping will largely close up the hole, but it will continue to weep. A thin wrapping of waterproof tape will complete a temporary repair until you can get a plumber in.

If your water piping is iron or steel (check with a magnet if you are not sure: lead or copper will not attract a magnet), there is a possibility that a pipe will have rusted through, or it may have sprung a leak at a joint. Even in a copper system soldered joints can spring a leak for no apparent reason. Again, use waterproof tape for a repair, but if this does not hold, something more permanent will be needed quickly.

If copper piping leaks at a compression joint, gently tighten the nut at the joint. You will need two spanners for this.

The inflow of water into the cold water cistern in the loft is regulated by a float or ball valve. If the washer of this becomes perished or worn or the valve sticks or otherwise fails to function properly, what should happen is that the water runs harmlessly away through the overflow pipe. (If you see water gushing out of the overflow pipe outside the house, it is a warning sign. If the cause is just a temporarily stuck float valve, flushing the w.c. may put it right. If water continues to run from the overflow pipe, climb into the loft to see if you can find the fault – if necessary, call a plumber.)

But if the overflow pipe should for some reason get blocked (for example, by a combination of spiders' webs and detritus), the water level in the cold water cistern will continue to rise until it slops over the top, and an appreciable amount of water finds its way on to the ceiling below.

Immediate action is to turn off the stop valve controlling the water supply to the cold water cistern. Then reduce the water level in the cistern by turning on taps upstairs (bath, basins) and flushing the w.c. until the water level in the cistern is low enough to let you clear the obstruction in the overflow pipe or the plumber work on the ball valve. It is not necessary to drain off more, and it is advisable not to do so.

An overflow pipe is usually short, running through the nearest wall. Pushing a thin cane or piece of wire through will clear it unless the stoppage is frozen water. If it is ice, warm the pipe if it is reachable; if not, you will have to wait for it to thaw.

If water leaks from the joint in a central heating pipe, put a bandage of waterproof tape around the joint as a temporary measure and get the leak dealt with by the installer or a plumber. A leak from the top of a radiator valve can often be tackled by lightly tightening the adjusting nut underneath the shield; on a valve with an 'O' ring seal, the seal may need to be replaced.

Rust developing on any part of a central heating installation should be taken as a warning that something is wrong; rust marks on pipes and radiators often indicate that there is a water leak. If you see a leak from the body of a radiator, isolate that radiator; you may need to get it replaced. If the pump starts to leak or fails to operate, the only sure cure is to have it replaced. This is a specialist job and involves draining off at least part of the system, and the subsequent refilling of it, adjustment of the pump and elimination of air locks.

leaks from rainwater

During a storm, wind may get underneath tiles or slates and break or remove them, allowing rainwater to get it. Usually you can hear it coming or see a damp patch appearing on the ceiling. These symptoms demand immediate action.

You need to get up into the roof space; it if is not floored, be careful to step only on joists and avoid stepping, standing or walking in the centre of joists (putting weight on the centre of a joist bows the timber and may crack the ceiling underneath). Putting a plank of wood across the joists spreads the person's weight.

Take with you a torch to see by, a bucket to put under the leak, a cloth or old towelling for mopping up, and some plastic sheeting (such as a plastic shopping bag or two). The bucket catching the water should preferably stand on a joist or joists, not on the ceiling plaster. It will get heavy as it fills and if it runs over, the water will soften the plaster it is standing on.

If only one or two tiles have come off and the hole through which the rain is coming is not too large, you may be able to stem the flow of water using the plastic bags. Tuck the edges of the plastic as tightly as possible underneath the tiles at the top of the hole and around the edges, and push it over the tiles at the bottom of the hole so that the water is directed farther down the roof. It is important that as much wind be kept out of the roof as possible; if wind gets into the roof space, it will take off more tiles.

If you cannot put up a barrier from within, telephone the fire brigade, tell them what has happened and hope they will come, equipped with a tarpaulin to put over the damaged section of the roof. Although it is an emergency to you, do not use the 999 emergency telephone number but dial the fire station's number.

As soon as possible, get a builder or roof repairer to come and renew that part of the roof.

Damp patches on the ceiling or drops of water coming through after persistent rain may be due to an insidious roof leak. Finding the source of such a leak may not be straightforward: water may come in at one place and run along roof timbers for a considerable distance, before it finds an easy path down on to the ceiling. If the easy path is along the electric wiring down to a ceiling light, or a switch, disconnect the circuit immediately by taking out the relevant fuse.

While it is raining, you will have to go up into the roof space armed with your torch, and try to trace the water back to its source. This may be a broken or dislodged tile, perished or damaged roof coverings, or a structural defect. Or the channel intended to take away the rainwater may be overloaded or obstructed.

Damp patches may appear on a wall if the flashing (the external waterproofing strip) between the chimney and the roof is defective. Your first inkling of trouble will probably be a damp spot appearing on a plastered wall adjacent to the chimney. Examination of the chimney stack in the roof space will normally reveal the path of the water. Remedying such a defect is a job best left to a builder or a roof repairer with suitable equipment.

Do not be tempted to ignore water cascading down the outside of the house from blocked gutters or downpipes. Although its effects are not immediate, damage to the structure of the house will follow if the fault is left for a long time.

Gutters and downpipes can get blocked by a build-up of leaves, debris which has fallen down from the roof, birds' nests, a tennis ball. Clearing gutters is usually a simple but tedious business involving the use of a ladder (or preferably a tower), a trowel, and a bucket to put the debris in. If there are a lot of trees around, this may need to be done once a year.

Clearing a downpipe is more involved. You may be able to reach the obstruction with a stick from the top and break it into pieces small enough to fall or be washed down to the bottom. If the downpipe is open at the bottom and delivers into a gully, you may be able to prod upwards and penetrate the blockage; or pushing a hosepipe up it (full bore fine jet) to reverse the direction of the normal flow may lift the blockage. If the pipe is not open at the foot but a manhole (inspection chamber) is nearby, it is possible that an entry pipe in it can be seen to come from the direction of the blocked rainwater pipe. If so, rodding or flushing with a hose thrust up to it may free it. Otherwise, a builder or plumber would need to be called in.

Unless the downpipe is cast iron, it may be possible to get at the blockage by removing sections of the pipe, starting at the bottom of the pipe and working up until the section with the blockage is found.

On older houses, the gully into which the downpipe pours may get blocked with leaves and other debris; clearing this away is simply a matter of scraping it all out.

through the external door
When the wind drives rain against and under the door, and penetrates to the insde to form a puddle of water, mop it up and stuff some cloth or old towels against the bottom of the door. To prevent it happening again, fit a weather board along the bottom of the door on the outside to conduct streaming water away from the foot of the door and a threshold board to prevent it from running underneath. These mouldings are stocked by timber merchants and usually sold in 1 metre pieces or may be cut for you to the required length. A soft wood is adequate for the weather board, but a hard wood is preferable for the threshold board because this will get more wear.

Fixing a draught excluding strip inside the jamb and lintel of the door will help to waterproof it by sealing the gap and preventing the wind from carrying in the rain. For fixing the strips, follow the manufacturer's instructions.

dripping tap

If a tap is dripping, it is probable that the washer is not making a watertight seal. This is most likely to be because the washer is worn, so the first thing to do is to change the washer.

Some water authorities will change washers free of charge, to stop the water being wasted (one drip a second wastes over 300 gallons a year). Some will deal only with cold taps that work directly off the main. (Some will also put new washers on leaking lavatory cistern float valves and on leaking storage cistern float valves.)

The very first issue of *Handyman Which?* November 1971, included the following instructions on changing a tap washer.

There are a number of different types of tap; the sort of tap you are

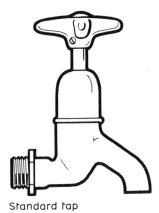

Standard tap

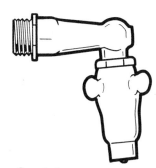

Supatap

most likely to have looks something like the British Standard tap. There are also Supataps which are designed to be simple to rewasher. All you have to do with these is to turn the tap on slightly, undo the nut above the finger grip with a spanner, and turn the tap nozzle until it comes away in your hand. Turn the nozzle upside down and bang it on a flat surface, and the washer and its mounting should fall out attached to the anti-splash device. Prise out the washer mounting; put in a new Supatap washer and put everything back together again.

Changing a washer on the British Standard tap is more difficult, but still fairly easy, provided you bear in mind the two golden rules of all plumbing:

- always get everything you need ready first: a pair of pliers and an adjustable spanner or wrench (preferably two), and a screwdriver if the tap handle is held on by a grub screw, a new washer and spare jumper
- shut off the relevant stop valve to the main supply or cistern.

To take the tap to pieces, you turn the handle into the fully open position first. This will drain off the water that is left in the pipes. You then have to lift off the handle and outside cover – you may have to undo a screw first.

If the cover is too tight to turn by hand, use your adjustable spanner; put a rag inside or some insulating tape around the tap so that you can grip the tap without scratching it. If it is still difficult to move, pour boiling water over it, or try a drop of penetrating oil.

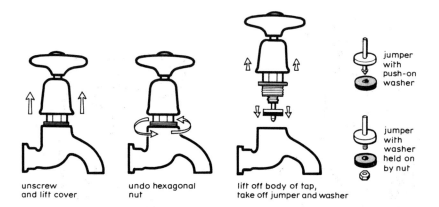

unscrew and lift cover | undo hexagonal nut | lift off body of tap, take off jumper and washer

jumper with push-on washer

jumper with washer held on by nut

Once you have moved the cover, you will see a nut on the body of the tap. Turn this with your spanner. If the tap is on a ceramic basin, you must be careful not to crack the basin by turning the spanner too hard if the nut is difficult to move. Take the strain with the second wrench or spanner.

Make sure you take out any loose broken bits of the old washer. The washer may be held on to the end of the jumper by a little nut or it may simply push on. If it is held by a nut and you find that the nut has corroded and will not turn, you will need to put in a new jumper complete with washer.

Put the tap together again, turn it to the shut position and then turn on the water supply. It is possible that the water will take a little while to come out.

If the tap goes on dripping, it may be because the surface (the seat) against which the washer is pressing is badly worn or pitted. A leaflet, *Plumbing in the home*, issued by the Institute of Plumbing includes the advice: 'If dripping persists, ask a plumber to reface the tap seating or insert a plastics reseating washer obtainable from builders' merchants.'

water not coming through

If you turn on the hot water tap and receive only a gurgling or hissing sound, the remedy may be no more than patiently waiting for someone at a lower level to turn off a tap there. But the cause is more likely to be an airlock in the plumbing: somewhere along the line a pocket of air has become trapped.

Airlocks can develop when refilling a system that has been drained. When refilling, proceed by stages: turn off the water at the hot water cylinder outlet, or at the incoming service pipe (rising main) if it is the plumbing of the cold supply which is affected. Open all taps to complete emptying. Then close all the taps to something under half way, to what would normally produce a slow flow. Turn on the supply. Go round the taps in turn and adjust each to give the same small even flow of water. This might require a couple of circuits because adjustment of one tap may affect the output of another. Then wait a bit and, starting at the lowest tap in the house, begin to open each tap the same amount – to half way, and by stages increasing the opening (but maintaining similarity between the taps) until the air has been expelled. Then turn each tap down to produce a mere dribble of water (again starting lowest first and working upwards). Finally, close all taps and all should be well.

frozen pipe
In winter time, your kitchen may be warm but the waste pipe which runs out of doors may have become frozen around its outlet, and cause a blockage.

Waste pipes rarely freeze in ordinary use – even cold water evacuates too quickly. Usually the problem starts with a dripping tap or trickling water, especially overnight. So, when freezing weather temperatures are expected, make sure that all taps are properly turned off. As an extra precaution, keep the sink or basin plug in its hole and, should you suspect the tap of an occasional dribble, put something under it to catch the drops. The object is to avoid allowing just a little water to pass through the pipe because this, trickling away only slowly, allows the freezing-up process to start.

A waste pipe generally freezes gradually and usually starts with an icicle outside. Applying a hot wet rag poultice or a hot water bottle should thaw a passage which can then be fully flushed out by running some hot water from inside. This is better than the drastic remedy of thawing it out by pouring a kettle of boiling water over it.

If the pipe runs along inside a cold external wall, the frozen blockage may extend back into the indoor part of the pipe. Thaw the pipe by applying a hot water bottle or hot wet cloth or by directing the flow from an electric hairdrier or fan heater set at 'warm' (not hot). Start thawing at the end nearest the tap.

If any pipe supplying the hot water system freezes, be sure to turn off the heat source – there could be an explosion if the boiler or heater is left on.

Because water expands when frozen, a pipe may crack during a freeze-up. If a pipe leaks when it thaws, turn off the stop valve on the pipe supplying it, and drain the cold water system. The Institute of Plumbing advises in this situation:

Do not open hot taps, as there could be a risk of the hot water cylinder collapsing if feed and vent pipes connected to it are frozen. Turn off central heating and let the fire in a solid fuel boiler die down. Switch off the electric immersion heater, if operating. Then call a competent plumber.

Once the pipe is empty, it may be possible to repair it by wrapping dry joint sealer (p.t.f.e. tape) over the split.

dry rot

Dry rot is a fungal affliction of timber exposed to damp conditions and starved of air. It develops in unventilated areas such as behind panelling or underneath floor boards. It can be recognised by a pungent smell of mushrooms, or may remain unnoticed until the floor boards give way. It is difficult to eradicate, and just covering up the hole will not be enough and will lead to further damage.

The fungus is extremely virulent, and can travel not only through timber but also over brickwork and concrete. Once established, it may spread quickly and weaken timber disastrously. Infected timbers and an appreciable area surrounding them should be cut out (and burned). Plaster should be chipped away; stone, concrete and especially brick must be vigorously scrubbed with a wire brush, and new preservatively treated timbers inserted.

There are various proprietary fungicidal preparations for dealing with the threat of further dry rot. A wide surrounding area (say, 10ft) must be treated with the chosen fluid.

There are specialist timber preservation firms who carry out treatment of dry rot. The inspection and report will be free, and a 20- or 30-year guarantee of the treatment should be given.

The British Wood Preserving Association (150 Southampton Row, London WC1B 5AL) offers advice on the treatment of timber damaged by dry or wet rot or by woodworm. It issues leaflets (send a large, stamped, self-addressed envelope for free literature) dealing with practical problems, including a general guide to preserving wood in home and garden, with safety precautions for the use and handling of preservatives. The Association can supply a list of member firms specialising in the remedial and curative treatment of timber.

blocked sink

A likely cause of a blocked-up sink is congealed fat holding debris which has passed the waste outlet grille and settled in the trap (where the pipe does a bend) or along the pipe.

To unblock a sink, first bale out as much of the water in the sink as possible, mopping up out of the plughole as much as can be reached. Then pour in neat liquid detergent or spoon washing soda down the plughole. (Do not use caustic soda crystals: water must never be poured on to dry caustic soda.) Pour a kettle of boiling water steadily down the outlet. If this penetrates the blockage and the liquid runs away, repeat the flushing with boiling water to carry off as much of the grease as possible.

If, however, the water stands in the sink, you will have to turn to more mechanical means. A plunger will shift most blockages. You must shut off the mouth of the overflow, otherwise the force will be lost; the side of your other hand or wet rags will do to plug this up. Use the plunger by placing it upright with the cup over the plughole, and then vigorously moving it up and down by the handle. You need an inch or two depth of water in the sink to work with. If the water level goes down, replenish and have another session with the plunger. Once the flow has been restored, cleanse the pipe with a thorough swill of boiling or very hot water.

If you do not have a plunger and the base of the sink is flat enough for your open hand to go over the plughole, try to achieve the effect of a plunger by pressing and raising the palm of your hand to create an alternation of compression and suction.

A more powerful alternative to the plunger is the jet action pump, similar to a bicycle pump but about twice the size with a T-shaped handle. The pump has to be filled with water, delivered through a jet nozzle with considerable pressure, which is likely to shift whatever has blocked the pipe. There is also a type using a cartridge of compressed air. Both types can be hired by the day.

You can attack the blockage from the other end by working something up the waste pipe from the outside (if accessible). Ordinary wire is not much good for this because it tends to bend and to stay bent so that it cannot be pushed in any great distance. There are purpose-made pipe clearing 'wires' – usually a length of flat spring steel with a small rounded knob or probe of hard metal fixed to the end. The flexible springy steel can be eased along by the leading knob and pushed past and around bends. Wear a pair of strong gloves when using one of these clearers to prevent the edges of the strip cutting your hand.

An improvised probe can be made from a length of coiled-spring stretchable curtain wire. An eyelet or a closed-up cup-hook securely screwed in the end will help its passage around bends.

If you still have not broken through, you will have to tackle the trap. The trap under the sink holds a little water to prevent air coming up from the drain gully with its attendant smell. (It also discourages insects entering by this route.) Although the trap is intended to hold just water, it also collects grease and other detritus too sticky and heavy to be carried over the bend by the water.

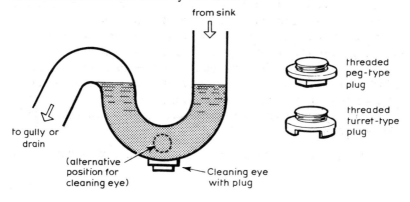

Older designs of trap are simply a bend in the pipe with a 'cleaning eye' closed by a threaded plug which can be unscrewed, at the bottom or side.

Before undoing the plug, place a bowl or bucket under the trap to catch the water and gunge that is going to come out.

Some plugs with a square peg need a spanner or wrench. For those with four upstanding lugs like the turrets of a castle, use the side edge of a screwdriver or spanner to get leverage on opposing pairs of lugs to turn the plug.

Remember that screws do up clockwise and undo anti-clockwise, but screws and threads upside down go the other way round to those of which you have a bird's eye view. There is very little thread on these plugs and their sockets, so care is essential to avoid damage by stripping a thread through over-tightening. If your plumbing is old metal piping and the plug has been undisturbed for years, there is the danger that in trying to get it undone, you will break the pipe, the plug, or both. Try chipping away old paint, treating with aerosol penetrating oil or applying heat. If you cannot cope, call in a plumber.

When the plug is out, you may find some sticky strands of tow or hemp around the thread, or a thin washer. Leave these undisturbed (unless you have replacements available) – they are there to help seal the plug when it is replaced.

A more modern sink may be fitted with a 'bottle' trap. With these, the

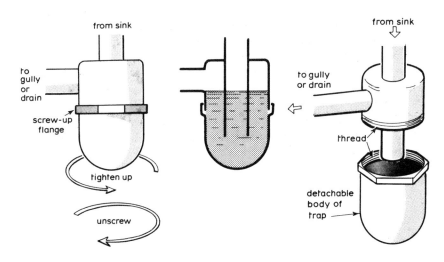

body of the bottle unscrews, or there is a cap at the bottom to unscrew. They should turn by hand pressure and not need a tool. As you release it, keep the part you are unscrewing upright because it will contain most of the debris that forms the blockage. Empty it and rinse it.

When the trap is open, ferret around in the downpipe and outlet pipe with a wire to get out anything you can, or probe through to make a clearway. Reassemble (do not over-tighten—no need to use a tool) and then flush through with hot water. This not only cleanses the pipe but is also essential in order to re-charge the sump in the trap with water.

In future, do not use the sink for getting rid of fats, tea leaves, vegetable peelings and such like. Do not empty the frying pan, roasting tin or gravy boat down the sink. To prevent fat setting, chase anything greasy down immediately with hot water. From time to time, douse through with boiling water and washing soda or a detergent. A good moment to do this is after the sink has been unused for a period – say, on returning home from a holiday: no water passing through for several days dehydrates and shrinks the built-up layer inside the pipe, loosening its hold. A copious whoosh through then will shift a surprising amount, and give you a clean start.

blocked gully
If waste water runs freely from the sink into the gully outside, but the gully itself overflows, the fault may lie there or in the drain beyond. To clear the gully of some of the accumulated debris and leaves, use a soup ladle or improvise something such as a small tin nailed to a stick. It is important to get the stuff out – not force it farther along the system, where the blockage may be much less easily removed. When you have got out all that you can with your ladle, you have the unpleasant task of putting your arm down the gully to feel around for things that may be down just around the bend. Wear a glove to protect your hand not just from dirt but from hidden sharp objects. Extract anything you find, then pour a bucket of water down to check whether the water drains away. If you have a garden hose, flush through before putting back the cover.

blocked w.c.

If your w.c. will not flush satisfactorily, there may be a blocked outlet at the trap or the pipe.

To unblock, start by baling out the lavatory pan if the water level has become high in it. It is preferable to retrieve whatever is blocking the trap, if this is feasible, rather than to push the obstruction farther on, since this may lead to trouble elsewhere. Reach in over and around the bend to feel whether you can get hold of the object to withdraw it. Do not be squeamish or tentative. Wear rubber gloves; adding a little hot water will warm the water in the bend a bit and a dash of disinfectant or pine essence will mask the odour if you find this offputting.

If you cannot find and remove the trouble, fish around farther with a piece of thick wire or curtain wire with a hook at the end. If that fails, use a rubber plunger, preferably the big version of the sink one. This has a collar to it to prevent inversion of the cup. Use an agitating push-and-pull action to alternate pressure and suction. This may do the trick even if the blockage is some distance away.

If the water level eventually goes down although clearance of the pan is very sluggish, take advantage of the fact that there is at least some passage of liquid past the obstacle. Let the pan empty as much as possible, allow time for the pipe to drain, then gently pour about 1 lb of caustic soda into the leftover water at the bottom of the pan. Then flush the solution down with a pail of boiling water, decanted in deliberately rather than vigorously, and let it stand. It may take an hour or two for the corrosive fluid to eat its way through the stoppage. Take care to protect the skin and eyes when using caustic soda.

There is a special long handled instrument for clearing lavatory pans and the pipes leading from them. It has a flexible shaft and a spiral attachment for extracting obstructions. It is available at hire shops.

unblocking from the outside
If you have not been able to reach the obstruction through the lavatory pan end, you will have to tackle the unblocking from the other end.

An inspection chamber outside, which can be identified by its metal or concrete lid set into the ground, is situated over a junction in the underground pipework. If there are several, start with the one nearest to the soil pipe. If whatever is causing the blockage is at or beyond that junction, you will see a foot or so of smelly fluid when you take off the cover. Use a clawed garden hoe or a rake to trawl around in this to try to find and dislodge the offending article. Do not use anything fragile which is likely to break and aggravate the situation.

If this preliminary probing fails to lower the fluid level, you will have to do something more methodical, using rods. With luck, someone somewhere in your community will have a set of drain rods, and lend them to you (promise to wash and disinfect them before you return them) or you can get them from a hire shop. A set of rods comes with sundry implements, one of which is a retrieving hook. This screws on to a rod in a clockwise direction. Each subsequent rod also screws on clockwise. It is of the utmost importance to screw each on very securely and always to continue turning the rods clockwise, throughout the operation. Should you turn them anti-clockwise, they will become uncoupled and the lengths beyond will be lost in the drain and cause a lot of trouble. For this job, you should wear old clothes and gloves.

An alternative unblocking tool that is for hire has a flexible shaft built up of steel wire bound round a supple core. It is worked by a small handle which rotates the shaft, driving it foward with a screwing action, negotiating bends en route like a snake, and piercing, gripping or pushing out any obstacles in its path.

The outlet from the junction that leads towards the main sewer is the one down which you should put the rods or snake. Continue twisting rods in a clockwise direction and putting on more rods until you feel the obstruction by an added resistance to forward motion of the prodder. When this happens, continue turning rods clockwise, but start pulling them back. If you are lucky, the retrieving hook will have engaged with the foreign body, and you will be able to drag it back to you. The rods will be exceedingly dirty; it is a great help if someone is standing by you with a hose or a watering can with which to clean the rods as they come back to you.

If the fluid level starts to drop in the inspection chamber, you will know that your troubles are largely over. If using a plunger on the end of the drain rods, beware of a sudden rush of water when clearance is effected—quickly withdraw the rods and plunger.

If you have failed to find the obstruction, you will have to go on to the next inspection chamber and repeat the process. If the next manhole is on your neighbour's land, you will have to ask him. If, however, your efforts continue to be unavailing, you will need to call in a plumber or professional drain clearing service. If you get up to the main sewer and find that is blocked, it is a matter for the local authority.

So much for the situation where the blockage is at or beyond a manhole. If the first inspection chamber is clear, however, this shows that the blockage is above that point. The most likely sites are at or near the exit trap of the w.c. pan or, in the case of an upstairs w.c., at the foot of the vertical soil pipe. So you have to try rodding back towards the house from the inspection chamber. Put something across the other outlet of the chamber, so that it will not block it but will prevent the freed obstruction from going through to block up the system farther down.

Blockages in the w.c. are preventable: they are brought about by misuse or mistake. A w.c. is not suitable as a general-purpose disposal unit. Many modern convenience articles are marketed as 'disposable'. Literally, this means that they can be thrown away after use but it does not necessarily warrant that they are soluble – indeed, some expand substantially on immersion. The bulkier kinds of sanitary towels, nappies and such like should be incinerated.

Children cause many blockages. It may be a landmark when a child can use the w.c. without assistance, but some discreet supervision is still desirable because many children go through a fastidious phase when nothing short of half a roll of lavatory paper satisfies their sense of hygiene. Followed by an ineffectual or omitted flushing, there is enough to create a blockage.

faulty cistern

If water flushes away from the lavatory pan but solid matter remains, allow the cistern to refill completely while you fill a bucket or a large bowl with water. Then flush the w.c. and at the same time pour the water from the bucket or bowl into the pan.

Wait until the cistern has refilled again, then check the water level inside. It should come up to about half an inch below the overflow outlet of the cistern. If there is not enough water in the cistern, adjust the ball float so that it allows more water to enter before cutting off the flow.

adjusting the float

The level at which the water supply is shut off can be adjusted by bending the arm to which the float is attached. It is not necessary to dismantle the float assembly to make this adjustment but it is important not to do it by straining the arm against the valve seating. If your fingers are not strong enough or there is insufficient space to get your hands in, clamp an adjustable spanner firmly on to the arm about an inch or so away from the valve. Only a slight bending or straightening of the bar will be needed to make the necessary adjustment so, to avoid over-correction, test the effect when you have felt the bar 'give' a little. The aim should be to get the water level about half an inch below the overflow pipe.

adjusting the flush

There are two kinds of mechanism for emptying a flushing cistern, the original bell type and the modern siphonic pattern. The bell type is usually mounted high up on the wall. A heavy iron bell sits in the sump of the cistern, with a little space under its rim to allow water inside it. A lever, hooked into a ring eye at the top of the bell, has its fulcrum on the edge of the cistern. A downwards pull on the chain attached to the outside end of the lever lifts the bell which sucks up some of the water in the sump; letting go of the chain allows the bell to fall back. When it returns by its own weight, the bell forces the water it contains over the outgoing funnel, setting up siphonage which empties the cistern. The height of the cistern, the bell and large bore of the delivery pipe combine to bring the water down with force to produce a strong flushing sluice.

There is little to go wrong with this simple mechanism in normal use. A sideways snatch on the chain, however, may unseat the fulcrum. Or the bell may be pulled out of vertical and go down awkwardly if impatiently yanked up and down before there is adequate water in the cistern. The remedy is to climb up and disengage the lever and lift the bell directly upwards. Do not try altering the posture in which it is lying; this may damage the walls of the cistern or the funnel of the

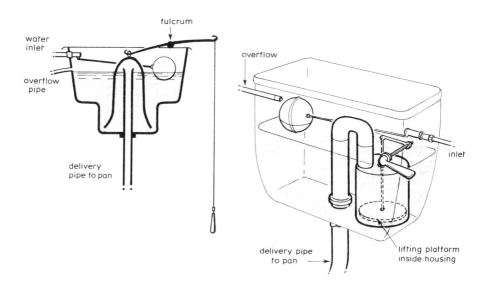

outgoing pipe. When you have lifted it, set the bell back upright in the sump, re-engage the hook of the lever into the top of the bell and drop the fulcrum lugs into their seatings. Do not be tempted to clean off any rusty encrustations you may see in the cistern: trying to remove them is likely to cause a leak.

The more modern siphonic cistern is usually mounted at low level and operated by a level handle. Depressing the handle lifts a platform housed in a casing. The platform is pulled up by a short arm connected via a square spindle to the lever handle. This raises water over the top of the outgoing pipe, which siphons off the rest of the water. Failure to deliver water may be due either to the link having come off or becoming loose on the spindle. To remedy this, hold the arm on to the spindle and undo the nut or screw one or two turns until the clamp is slack. Move the arm along the spindle until it is directly over the platform and then re-clamp.

overflowing
The amount of water admitted to the cistern is controlled by the air-filled floating ball which presses a washer in a piston block against the

mouth of the water inlet pipe when the water level has reached the desired height. If it does not float properly, the water will continue to come in. If you see water coming out from the overflow pipe on the cistern, look inside for the fault. A ball that will not surface or floats too low in the water probably has water inside it and has become too heavy to be buoyant. It may be possible to mend or seal a hole in the float but it is simpler and not more expensive to replace the ball. However, you may have to do an emergency repair, meanwhile. Turn off the water supply to the cistern, then unscrew the float to free it from the arm, or take out the complete arm and float if they are in one piece.

Empty as much water out of the ball as possible. It really needs two holes, one to drain off the water, the other to let air in, and it may be necessary to enlarge a hole a little. Dry the ball well, then mend the hole with epoxy resin or plug it by inserting a self-tapping screw (not too tightly turned). A hole too large for this can be covered with a waterproof medical sticking plaster from the first-aid kit. Press the plaster on with the thumb nail to get close adhesion, then seal over and all round with a coat of nail varnish, oil-based paint or epoxy resin, and allow to dry thoroughly before returning to use.

Where time or circumstances do not permit this repair, a perforated float can be temporarily put back into action, after emptying, by enclosing it in a plastic bag with the mouth of the bag wrapped and tied round the lever arm.

Where the reason for overflowing is not a faulty float, the cause may be an obstruction at the water inlet preventing the valve from closing properly, or a bit of grit on the washer, or an old or defective washer. A worn washer probably gives some notice of the defect by intermittent dribbling at the overflow pipe over a period of time. A sudden onset of overflowing is likely to be the result of an obstruction. The local water undertaking's emergency service may be willing to deal with this because such faults cause water wastage. If not, change the washer or, if you cannot cure the fault, call in a plumber.

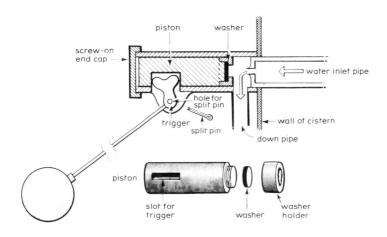

putting in new washer on ball valve in cistern

You will need:
small screwdriver (to use for prodding and leverage)
small stillson wrench (to hold with)
adjustable spanner (to undo/turn with)
pliers (to close up/undo with)
fine steel wool (to clean surfaces)
petroleum jelly (to lubricate screw threads)
plastic knitting needle (for poking with)
new washer (leather, rubber or neoprene; ask at hardware shop for ball valve washer; standard size)
spare brass split pin (in case existing one not reusable)

- turn off water supply at stop valve
- if working on w.c. cistern, flush to get water out of it; if working on cold water storage cistern, turn on a few taps to lower water level
- unscrew end cap of piston
- withdraw split pin: use pliers to close split end, then take pin out with a straight pull so as to leave pin undistorted and fit for re-use
- remove trigger from slot: downward pressure may suffice or you may have to jiggle it about a bit before it will free
- insert small screwdriver into slot and ease piston out (if assembly

undisturbed for years, an encrustation may have built up beyond normal movement point: scrape it out with a penknife)

- clean outside of piston with soaped steel wool—this should reveal the joint line between main block and washer holder
- unscrew washer holder to release washer (if it is stubborn, hold main body firm (if using a wrench, put a piece of stout card between the jaws to avoid scoring the brass body) and use stillson wrench or pliers (also with card to protect) on washer holder to unscrew it; alternatively, dip washer holder end of piston into boiling water for about 30 seconds and then unscrew)
- lever out old washer (use screwdriver, if necessary) and scrape away any residue or dirt around its seating
- fit in new washer (or, in emergency, turn old one over)
- smear the thread on end of piston and in washer holder with petroleum jelly, and screw back on (use no more than firm hand pressure, so that it will be easy to undo next time)
- burnish inside of piston housing with soaped steel wool, then wipe out thoroughly with clean rag
- take a knitting needle (plastic, to avoid damaging nozzle) and gently insert it into and through the water supply inlet to free any obstruction there may be
- put back piston into housing: washer end first, with slot downwards
- insert trigger arm
- replace split pin (old one should be cleaned smooth first); open up ends to a narrow V
- smear thread of screw for end cap with petroleum jelly, screw cap on, finger-tight only
- turn on water supply
- check water level when cistern filled: it should be about $\frac{1}{2}$ inch below overflow pipe.

If the piston cannot be dismantled, you will have to dig out the old washer from the nozzle end. Do this with a small screwdriver and scrape the recess of the holder to get out any residue or dirt. Put a smear of petroleum jelly into the recess to help new washer seat properly. Then manipulate the new washer into place, using the screwdriver inserted at an oblique angle to push down round the edges, taking care not to cut or abrade the washer.

septic tank

If your house is not connected to the main sewer but relies on a septic tank and the system becomes clogged, effluent will back up and hinder the draining of sinks and w.c., or it may overflow (accompanied by vile smells). The situation may arise due to some change of domestic routine, such as the arrival of a baby involving the use of quantities of detergents, sterilising preparations and the like. Also, when a house is left unoccupied for some period during which the bacterial colony in the septic tank is reduced, it may not work again efficiently at first when the house is occupied again.

To drench the tank in disinfectant is not the remedy. This may kill the offensive odour but will also massacre the micro-organisms on which the bacterial breakdown process relies. Having the tank pumped out (unless this is already overdue) would give only a temporary alleviation.

What is required is to renew the bacterial colony and to restore its natural bio-degrading activity by putting a dose of special cesspool cleaning powder (obtainable from chemists, hardware shops and some horticultural suppliers) into the w.c. pan, with about half a gallon of lukewarm water. Allow half an hour for generation, and then flush. The powder is non-caustic and non-toxic, so no special precautions are needed provided that the manufacturer's instructions are followed.

A septic tank will not function indefinitely without attention. Treat it with respect: do not send down grease, fats and oils, be sparing with detergents and sterilising preparations. Keep the ventilation to the tank free from obstructions. As a safety precaution, if you lift the lid to inspect the interior, do not have any naked flame nearby: volatile vapour may have built up and reached a combustible state.

Fire

It will be too late to turn to this section of the book for reference when you have to contend with an outbreak of fire. Read it now, and be prepared.

Take a deliberate walk around your home, stand in each room and consider how you would reach safety from it if there were a fire in that room, and also what you would do if you were in that room when a fire broke out elsewhere in the building. Work out the best route, and an alternative if that should be blocked. Remember that you may have to escape in the dark – a fire may fuse your electricity supply or the smoke may prevent you from seeing – so practise moving blindfold.

The most lethal element in a fire is the smoke not the flames. Toxic fumes and vapour can kill by asphyxiation before flames can inflict fatal burns. Closed doors hold back smoke. It is a basic rule to shut the door where a fire has started. Do not go back in. Even a small initial fire may develop rapidly and the smoke created can be fatal.

escaping from fire

If you are caught in a room and a fire has broken out outside it, regard the closed door as a shield and do not rush to open it in a panic. Feel whether the door is warm, and do not open it if you can feel heat at any level. If you think it is safe to open the door, do so with caution.

Do not stand at the opening edge of the door ready to peer through the gap when the door is opened. The rush of flames or hot gases into the room may be instantaneously incapacitating.

in preparation

Because it is difficult to predict how anyone will behave in the sudden emergency of a fire in the home, it is important to have established some form of fire drill, particularly where there are children or elderly people. Everyone in the household should be made to understand the essential actions:

● to escape
● to isolate a fire.

Choose an assembly point outside and away from the house, and make sure everyone (including overnight guests) knows where this is, so that you can check whether anyone is missing.

It would be wise to make a routine tour of the house before going to bed every night, to check that all is safe. Begin by switching the TV off at the set, and unplug it before you go to bed. Check that fires are safe and cooker switched off, and unplug electrical appliances. Make sure that no smouldering cigarette ends have been left in ashtrays or anywhere else. Shut windows and doors. Look to see that the key for unlocking the front door is accessible, and that the bolts or latches on other external doors can be moved easily.

water

Water is the best extinguishing agent in most cases. It not only cools but cuts off oxygen and inhibits the spread of flame. Where there is no accessible water tap nearby, it may be worth having a large jug or a vase with a handle permanently ready on, say, a window ledge at the end of a corridor – and keep it filled.

fire-smothering cloths

A fire-smothering cloth or blanket is a useful standby in a kitchen emergency, especially for a chip pan fire. Such blankets can be bought folded into a quick-release metal box which, at a touch, drops the blanket into the hand, or folded into a hanging pack from which it is pulled out. The cloth should open out to be about a metre square and have two tabs to provide a protective hand-hold.

Fix the container at about eye level in a prominent position – for instance, near (but not over) the cooker out of the reach of children. Do not attach it to a door.

sand

Fine dry sand is a good smotherer of fire: it pours like water but more slowly and it stays in place without running or seeping away. But it is heavy. It is easiest managed in a handled container, such as a bucket or a coal hod. A good place to keep it is some two or three feet above floor level on a shelf or hung on a strong bracket. The height saves having to make the initial lift when needed and it leaves the floor clear.

Sand can be obtained from garden shops, and builders' merchants; if taken from the seashore or dunes, it may need to be sifted through a sieve to remove particles of debris.

fire extinguishers

The British Standard for portable fire extinguishers is BS 5423:1980. Some extinguishers complying with the BS also carry the FETA (Fire Extinguishing Trades Association) and FOC (Fire Offices' Committee) label of approval.

Small disposable fire extinguishers of the aerosol type, intended for emergency use in kitchen, garage or car, are covered by BS 6165:1981.

An extinguisher should be installed in a visible, accessible position.

It is essential to study the manufacturer's instructions and to be sure that you know how the appliance is intended to be used so that vital time is not lost reading how to operate the extinguisher when a fire has broken out. If the manufacturer has recommendations about how to keep the appliance in good working order, these should be strictly followed.

Some of the smaller extinguishers do not contain enough to be of much use on anything but a small fire.

A fire extinguisher will not help you unless you know how to use it and what to use (and not to use) it on. There is a recommended colour code for the canister, indicating the extinguishing agent:

extinguishers

colour of canister	extinguishing agent inside	use for
black	carbon dioxide	almost all types of fire including electrical apparatus but not on oil-burning heater; not suitable for use in small area; non-toxic
blue	dry powder	spilt flammable liquids such as petrol and paraffin; can be used for chip pan fire; messy; can damage equipment and furniture
cream	foam	flammable liquids such as oils, spirits and fats; messy; can damage equipment and furniture
green	vapourising liquid (halon)	almost all types of fire, including electrical apparatus; intended for use in large areas
red	water	any free-burning fire such as wood, cloth, paper; NOT for electrical apparatus or flammable liquids such as oils, spirits, fats; can be used on oil-burning heater; harmless and non-toxic.

Note The British Standards now recommend that water extinguishers are coloured red, and all other extinguishers predominantly red but with the colour for the extinguishing agent (black, blue, cream, green) readily apparent.

outbreak of fire

The order of priorities is

- raise the alarm
- contain the fire as much as you can do safely; close doors and windows of the room where the fire is, if you can
- call the fire brigade
- evacuate all people (and pets, if possible) from the premises
- notify the neighbours if your property is not detached.

To call the fire brigade, all you need do is dial '999' (no coins needed in a call box) and ask for FIRE. When you are put through, give the address clearly, with brief directions if the house may be difficult to find. Say if there is anyone trapped.

When a fire breaks out, particularly if you are alone at the time, personal safety and summoning the fire brigade are the main priorities. Never hesitate about calling the fire brigade – precious early minutes give them a much better chance of tackling the blaze successfully, and they will not mind if, on their arrival, the fire has gone out of its own accord or been extinguished.

When you have called the fire brigade, stay clear. Do not go back into a burning room or house, and keep everyone else outside.

Do not go back to rescue any object or valuable from a room where the fire has caught hold: even if the flames do not seem very fierce, the smoke and fumes may overcome you before you realise what has happened.

If there is a person trapped within, do not risk you own life by charging back into the room or house; opening doors or windows may well aggravate the fire and thus injure the person you are trying to rescue as well as yourself. Direct the firemen to the victim, and tell them of any alternative way of approach if the obvious one is blocked by the fire.

trying to put out a fire

Only if the fire is small and can be safely and easily contained should you attempt to act yourself.

Stand as far back from the flames as you can, and keep clear of smoke.

Do not place yourself so that there is fire between you and your escape route.

Do not try to drag burning articles away from the fire – this will spread the blaze and may burn you.

using water as an extinguisher
Pour water deliberately over or at the flames, working from the outside edge of the burning area towards the centre so that you drive the flames back rather than forcing them onwards. This makes more effective use of a bowl or bucket of water than dashing the whole lot in the general direction of the fire in one go.

You could use the garden watering hose if it is within reach and ready for use. (But if it is not, do not go off to get it: summon the fire brigade first.) Open the tap to which the hose is connected to full pressure, and, if the hose is fitted with a nozzle, turn it to give a sharp jet that will carry distance with power. Bring the stream to bear on drenching and cooling the periphery of the flames, working inwards to the centre of the fire.

Never use water on any electrical apparatus that is still plugged in: water conducts electricity and the appliance may become live and the water may conduct the electricity back to and through you.

And do not pour water on to burning oil in a pan: it will cause the flames to erupt and the flaming oil will be dispersed, floating on the water, and spread the fire.

Water can be used for fire from an oil-burning heater, but stand at least six feet away when throwing or spraying the water on to the burner. If possible, continue spraying or throwing buckets of water to cool it down and prevent re-ignition.

frying pan and chip pan fire

Do not attempt to move a blazing frying pan or chip pan. Trying to get rid of the fire by throwing it out of the house, through the door or window, is dangerous: in manoeuvring the hot and heavy pan, you risk slopping boiling hot fat or oil over yourself and the surroundings, setting yourself alight or setting fire to the curtains or other furnishings. Leave it where it is and tackle it there.

Cut off the heat source by switching off the gas or by switching off the electric current at the cooker socket on the wall (if it is safe to do so) as well as, or instead of, the control knob.

Never use water at close quarters on an oil or fat fire. Water on the flaming oil or fat would spread the flame and there would be a shower of burning fat.

To smother the flames, try to cover them. If you have a fire-smothering cloth, pull it out and use it: hold it at an angle to the flames (so that it shields you). If you do not have one, cover the pan instantly with any thick cloth. Even a dry one will retard and confine the flames momentarily, while you get another cloth wetted and brought to reinforce the smothering action.

Or place a big plate or lid, larger than the frying pan, over the pan. But do not go off searching for one: whip off a lid from any pan on the stove, give it a quick sharp shake or rap it against some hard surface to get rid of droplets of condensation. The best way of putting a plate or lid over the burning pan is to hold it upright between you and the pan; touching the lower edge of the plate or lid against the nearside rim of the pan, lower it over. This prevents flames fanning out towards you. Do not hold on to the lid or try dobbing it about to catch any escaping tongues of flame. If a chopping board is handy, use that.

Once you have managed to smother a chip pan fire, keep the pan covered until cool – if you uncover too quickly, the fat will re-ignite. If you cannot put the flames out, abandon – shut all doors and windows if time allows, get out and shut the door behind you. Call the fire brigade.

HOW NOT TO HAVE A CHIP PAN FIRE

- Dry chips. If you do not have time to let them drain before frying, lay them on a dry tea towel, sprinkle with salt, fold over the cloth and lightly rub them, then shake them out into a colander. (A little salt adhering will give a crispy coloured finish to the chips when cooked.)

- Use no more oil or fat than necessary: do not fill the chip pan more than one-third full of oil.

- Do not overheat the oil or fat. When fat starts smoking, it is reaching the point of spontaneous combustion and the heat must be turned off immediately.

- Tip chips in gently: do not throw them in with a splash; lower chip basket slowly. Do not empty frozen chips straight in from the bag.

- **Never leave the pan unattended:** most fires occur when the person who is doing the cooking is out of the kitchen.

On an electric cooker, always switch each individual control off fully when not in use. If switched off only at the wall socket, someone else may switch on and unwittingly heat up a ring on which a pan is standing.

aerosols
Do not place an aerosol on a heated surface and do not throw an empty container into a fire to dispose of it.

Do not use any aerosol in the vicinity of a flame, even a pilot light, or radiant electric heating element, or while smoking. Do not light a match when you have just used an aerosol (such as a perfume spray).

adhesives and solvents
The vapour from adhesives and fixatives is flammable, even explosive – with the risk of accidental ignition. So, make sure there is plenty of ventilation when using adhesives manufactured from petroleum or acetates, and no naked flame nearby nor hot wires (such as in an electric toaster or heater), and no smoking. Extend these precautions to adjacent rooms: the fumes can catch alight from a flame at a considerable distance from the point where the adhesive is in use.

A fire from the vapour of such products as adhesives, paint thinners and strippers or solvent cleaning fluids, is likely to be intense, widespread and accompanied by toxic fumes. Get out at once, closing doors behind you, and call the fire brigade. On their arrival, explain briefly what has occurred.

bottled gas
If you have to summon the fire brigade to deal with any fire, tell them if you have a container of gas on the premises, even when this is not the cause or is not at the site of the blaze.

A leaflet issued by the Fire Protection Association in conjunction with the Liquefied Petroleum Gas Industry on fire safety with LPG appliances says

Accidents most frequently occur as a result of gas leaking when people are assembling appliances or changing cylinders or cartridges. A small leak can produce a large volume of highly flammable gas. The gas is heavier than air so that it collects near the floor or ground and can be ignited at a considerable distance from the source of the leak. If the escaping gas is ignited in a room or other space there may be a fire and an explosioin.

Do not smoke and make sure there are no flames (such as pilot lights) or working electrical appliances in the vicinity when connecting or changing cylinders or cartridges.

If possible assemble appliances or change cylinders or cartridges in the open. If the appliance is not easily portable, open windows and doors to give good ventilation.

Test for leaks by applying soapy water to all joints and connections. Never use a lighted match or any other flame.

gas heater
The fire danger with any gas appliance is a build-up of an explosive mixture of gas due to tardy initial ignition, to leaving the gas turned on unlit, or to a simple leak.

Tardy ignition means too much gas is released at the jets before the gas lights. Symptoms are a pause of several seconds before ignition – which occurs with a noisy woomph. The danger is that delayed lighting may cause a blow-back and a flaming explosive pocket of gas mixture around the appliance, singeing the user and setting fire to curtains or other things in the vicinity. If there is unduly delayed ignition, turn off and wait until ventilation has removed all trace and smell of gas before trying again.

If the cause is an inadequate pilot light or sluggish burner jet due to dirt, it needs to be cleared and cleaned by a gas serviceman. All gas appliances should be serviced regularly.

in the living room

The material (foams, plastics and other synthetic fabrics) of some modern furniture, if it catches fire, gives off large amounts of dense toxic smoke and burns rapidly. Action must be swift: get everyone out of the room, shut the door, and call the fire brigade. Even if you think a fire is out in a piece of furniture, call the fire brigade—it may be smouldering. Do not under any circumstances attempt to take the furniture outside: fresh air may cause it to re-ignite.

Traditional upholstered furniture (with timber framing and padding of natural fibres) ignites less readily and burns more slowly, with less smoke. You may have time to get water or a fire extinguisher to it. Do not lift cushions or attempt to take off loose or fitted covers: this would let in more air and turn smoulder into flames.

If, when you return to the room after fetching some extinguishing material, you find that the fire has begun to flare or to make a lot of smoke, abandon the attempt, shut the door to the room, and wait for the firemen.

If soot in a flue or chimney catches alight, it will not help, and is too late and dangerous, to rake out the fire. Shut any air inlets, and close draught dampers, shut the doors and windows of the room, and call the fire brigade.

An open fire should have a guard; a close-meshed guard prevents sparks from flying out into the room. It defeats the purpose of a fireguard to use it as a drying rack for clothes.

A heater placed too near to furniture or unintentionally switched on when out of sight may cause a fire. An electric heater should never be tidied away behind furniture while still plugged in. Do not use a time switch for a radiant fire.

Trailing flex is a trip hazard but it is not a safe solution to tuck flex away under the carpet because the friction from walking over it may fray the insulation and cause a short circuit and/or unsuspected slow ignition.

If there is any fire involving electrical equipment, switch off, unplug at the socket, disconnect at the main fuse box – whichever is the quickest and safest to do. Do not use water or a fire extinguisher until the appliance is disconnected.

tv set

Television sets employ high voltages and some parts generate considerable heat. Space all around a set and ventilation around any grilles is essential. It should never be covered by drapery.

There may be localised overheating within the set, so if you notice a peculiar smell similar to that of burning rubber or plastic, switch off, unplug and call the television engineer to investigate.

Fire in a tv set may start gradually and not break out until after the set has been switched off. Should even the smallest wisp of smoke be seen coming from the set, take instant action. Switch off and disconnect and call the fire brigade. If a television set burns, the fire will be fierce with toxic fumes and a risk of explosion.

Throwing water on an overheated set may cause the tube to implode. Get a blanket, rug, or large bath towel (wet if possible) and throw it over the set to prevent any flames spreading and limit the danger from flying glass. Stand clear and do not investigate under the blanket; leave this to the firemen.

clothes on fire

If someone's clothing catches fire, the priority is to stop the flames by smothering.

If your own clothes catch fire, do not run about. Lie down, straighten out and roll sideways across the floor; to and fro if there is not much space. If there is a rug, bedspread, coat, heavy curtain or any thick non-flammable material reachable, roll up in it to suffocate the flames. Do not sit up or stand erect again until you have dealt with any clothing that is still smouldering. It is an instinctive reaction to use the hands as beaters but protect them as much as possible; wrap them up, thrust them into socks, slippers, anything available to take the brunt of direct contact with burning material.

If it is another person whose clothing is on fire, get the person down flat and horizontal immediately, with the burning part uppermost. Do not roll him or her round – rolling is only for the person in flames who is alone, with no one to do the smothering. Use a rug, coat or any similar thick materials to smother the flames – keep it between the flames and the person's face and head.

On no account attempt to get burning or burnt clothes off the person; douse in cold water. Get medical attention as quickly as possible.

electric blanket
Follow the instructions that come with a new blanket about correct use and storage; for instance, not folding the blanket on itself or putting a heavy weight on it while it is switched on.

If a defective blanket overheats and sets fire to the bedding, do not open the windows of the room to get rid of the smoke. First, unplug. Do not open the bed to discover the extent of burning or damage because this will let air into it and turn smoulder into flame. Call the fire brigade. Then, if it is safe to do so, take water to the bed and drench it thoroughly.

Never smoke in bed.

garage
If there is an outbreak of fire in the garage, get the car out immediately if it is safe to do so. Call the fire brigade, and limit your fire-fighting efforts to the best that can be done straightaway. If you cannot quickly bring the flames under control, get out immediately, closing the doors behind you, if you can.

Tell the firemen what combustibles there are inside the garage, especially any pressurized containers, chemicals, paint or a can of petrol.

bonfire
Do not have a bonfire where sodium chlorate has been used as weed-killer. And do not have a bonfire when there has been a long dry spell.

Be careful about burning dry autumn leaves: they may take off in the rising air currents and rain down, still burning, over a wide area.

The radiant heat of a bonfire can cause damage to nearby trees, shrubs, hedge, shed and fence, and flying sparks and embers may set them alight. It is as well to damp these by hosing them down before lighting the fire.

Keep a bucket of water handy (on the windward side of the fire) or have the hosepipe connected to a tap, ready for emergency use.

Do not leave a bonfire smouldering; douse it thoroughly with water and put a few shovelfuls of earth on the embers.

being burgled

If you find that your home has been burgled, telephone for the police, or get someone else to do this for you. This is a '999' occasion.

Touch nothing, or as little as possible, to safeguard any fingerprints there may be. The place left as it is (not tidied up or straightened) may suggest a recognisable mode of operation to the investigating police.

If credit cards, cheque books or travellers cheques are missing, notify the issuing bank or company immediately. If keys have been stolen or used, the locks should be changed. Lodge a claim with your insurance company without undue delay; do not wait to see whether valuables are recovered.

The Consumer Publication *Securing your home* describes in detail what to do when you have been burgled – and how to try and prevent it.

Windows

A broken window pane demands immediate action. The first thing to do is to sweep up the big bits of glass, then carefully vacuum clean the entire area so that slivers are not picked up by children and pets. A damp rag wiped over the area will effectively deal with tiny splinters; the complete rag should be thrown (in a plastic bag) into the dustbin. Wear gloves.

Metal windows are tricky for an amateur to replace – you may need to have specialist help.

If you measure the size of the frame into which the new piece of glass will have to go before it is cleared of glass, measure the entire frame area – not just to the edge of putty. It would be better to clear out all the glass before attempting to measure up for a replacement. But that would leave a wide open hole (cold in winter and a security risk).

A window pane has to be replaced from the outside, so if the broken one is upstairs, a ladder is needed – and unless you are used to working on and from a ladder, do not attempt it. Get a glazier or builder.

putting in a new pane

If you do attempt it yourself, first you have to remove from the frame all fragments of the old glass. Put on stout gardening type leather gloves. Save a largish piece (wrap it safely) to take to the glass merchant for matching when you buy the new glass.

Try to pull out remaining pieces of glass in line with the pane, but do not pull too hard: if the glass comes out with a rush, your arm might fly back and get impaled on jagged fragments on the other side of the frame. If the putty is old and hard, you may be able to soften it with paraffin, or you may have to chip out the glass and also the putty with hammer and chisel (if you have protective goggles, put them on).

Work from the outside to chip all the old putty out. If the glass is held in by wood beading, prise this up carefully first, starting in the centre of a long side, and keep it for putting back afterwards. Remove any old glazing sprigs and scrape out all the old putty from the rebate, right back to bare wood or metal.

In a metal-framed window, the glass is held in by metal clips. Take these out, mark the position of the holes on the edge of the frame and save the clips to put back in again later.

Make quite sure that you have removed all traces of old putty and broken glass, then smooth the window frame with coarse sandpaper, and apply a coat of the primer paint appropriate to the material of the frame. If the exposed wood is damp, paint it with spirit-based knotting liquid.

Measure the height and width of the window frame to the nearest 1/16th of an inch (or 1mm if your tape is metric). It is better to use a steel rule than a dressmaking tape.

Subtract 1/8th of an inch (or 3mm) from each measurement. There must be adequate clearance for the glass – to allow for small movements in the frame. If the window is an unusual shape, cut a piece of cardboard to the shape, and take it with you to the shop.

Most towns have a glass specialist shop, so look up 'glass merchants' in the Yellow Pages telephone directory; failing that, a hardware shop or ironmonger may sell glass.

A glass merchant stocks a range of clear and patterned glass and will usually cut it to size for you while you wait. Show the glass merchant the broken piece you have brought with you; he will be able to identify the type and thickness you need. For patterned glass, you must specify which way the pattern runs.

While you are there, buy also putty: metal casement putty or, for wooden windows, linseed oil putty and glazing sprigs (small tapered headless tacks). Allow about 5oz of putty per foot of frame and get about 1lb extra because you are likely to waste some.

Before putting in the new putty, you have to prepare it: take some in your hand and knead it until it is warm and soft. If the putty is too oily to work, knead it first on a piece of newspaper which will absorb some of the oil. If it is too hard, beat it out flat like pastry and sprinkle a few drops of linseed oil on it, then knead.

Then press the putty bit by bit into the sides and back of the rebate with your thumb to make a firm bed about 1/4 inch thick all round the frame. Put in the new pane (bottom end first so you do not drop it) and press it firmly into the putty all round. Push at the edges of the glass, not in the centre. The putty will be squeezed out on the inside of the pane.

Secure the pane by tapping the sprigs into the side of the frame, using a small hammer carefully. You want the sprigs to be covered by putty, so tap each in until it is about 1/8th inch inboard of the frame. Put sprigs in at about 12-inch intervals; about 9-inch intervals for a small pane. With a metal window frame, replace the clips at this stage.

Trim away the excess putty from the inside of the pane, at a slightly sloping angle. Then press in more putty around the outside of the pane so as not to leave any gaps. Smooth down with a knife so that it looks like the other frames.

If there is beading to be put in, prime it before putting it in and apply less putty against the pane. Press the beading firmly into place and fix it to the frame with long (panel) pins. Shape the edges of the putty to a slight angle.

Finish off by running over the putty inside and outside with a moistened soft paint brush to seal it to the glass. Clean off all the putty marks from the pane with methylated spirit (but do not let it get on to the putty).

Leave the window for about two weeks so that the putty can dry out before you paint the frame. Putty goes on shrinking, so paint on the outside over the putty up to the glass to seal the joint and stop water getting into any cracks.

broken sash cord

A sash window consists of two sashes (framed panes of glass) of equal size which slide up and down past each other. They are suspended by sash cords, nailed at one end to the sash, running over pulleys at the top of the window frame, and attached to heavy metal weights which counter-balance the sashes. These weights hang in the hollow space behind the frame – called the weight-box.

When one sash cord breaks, one side of the sash is unsupported, so it is more difficult to move and may jam. If both cords break, the window will not stay poised where you want it; if it is up at the moment the second cord breaks, the sash may fall violently.

If one of the cords is fraying or has broken, it is a good idea to replace all four cords – they may be worn with use or rotten with lack of use. If you can do one, doing four does not involve much extra work.

To remove the old cord, work on the inner sash first. Lower it to the bottom of the window. If the cord is not already broken, cut it close to the top of the sash, holding tightly on to the upper cut end; you will get a better grip with a pair of pliers – the weight is surprisingly heavy. Let the weight down gently.

To free the sash from the frame, remove the beading on the room side of the window at each side. First, break any film of paint by running a sharp tool from top to bottom between the bead and the frame, then prise out the bead, starting at the middle and bowing it so that it springs out. Take out the old panel pins. Mark the right and left beads, since they may not be interchangeable.

Now lift out the inner sash from the frame. You may need some help for this if you are dealing with a large, heavy sash. Before you can take out the outer sash, you have to remove the parting bead that separates the two sashes. Finally, lift out the outer sash. Mark both sashes so that you can tell which is which.

The weight-box cover is usually a push fit, but may be held in by nails or screws. Take out the weight and remove the old cord. Use an old screwdriver to lever out the knot – it can be awkward. The weights for the top and bottom sashes may be different – do not mix them up.

Now remove the rest of the cord from the groove at the side of the sash. It may have a patent fixing which releases fairly readily; there are more likely to be nails or staples which have to be pulled with pincers or pliers.

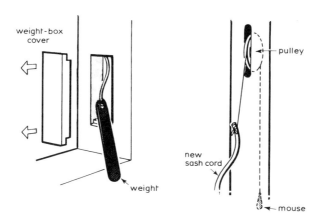

Smooth off any roughness (bits of old paint, for instance) on the part of the window frame where the sashes run, and on the sides of the sashes themselves. Rub them with sandpaper and then with a candle or a dry bar of soap to wax the surfaces.

Check the pulleys and clean them up; lubricate them if they need it. It may be an opportunity to suck out dirt and debris from the weight box with a vacuum cleaner.

putting in the new cord
Sash cord (generally waxed hemp or braided cotton) is sold in hardware shops and builders' merchants usually in 12 ft lengths. For a 6 ft high window, you would need 24 ft to do all the four cords. Take a piece of the old cord to the shop to make sure you get the correct size. You will also need broad headed nails, 1 inch long, for nailing down the new cord on to the sash, and panel pins for nailing down the beading.

To put in the new cord, you need a small weight, referred to as a 'mouse' (any small heavy object which can be passed over the pulley), attached to a piece of string the height of your window. Tie the other end of the string to the end of the sash cord.

Feed the mouse and string over the pulley so that it can drop down inside the weight-box. Let the mouse carry the string down to the bottom of the box. Push the new cord over the pulley and pull it down with the string. Untie the string (also take out the mouse).

Thread the new sash cord into the top of the weight and knot the end tightly with a non-slip knot. Push the knot right into the hole in the weight so that nothing sticks out to prevent the weight running freely up and down.

Put the weight back into the box and pull the other end of the cord until the weight moves up to the very top of the box. Then let it down about two inches.

You now need to keep it there while you attach the other end of the cord to the sash to get the length of the cord right. The simplest way to do this is to tack the cord to the inside of the frame just below the pulley. (Do not drive the tack home too hard – it is there only temporarily.)

Get to this stage for all four sash cords before nailing the cord to the sash. First, work on the outer sash.

To get the length of new cord right, stand the sash in position at the bottom of the window frame and mark the cord where it comes to the bottom end of the groove in the side of the sash. Cut it there. Then put the cord down the groove and nail it in position with broad headed nails. The last nail should not be right at the top of the groove but below the bottom edge of the pulley, otherwise the top nail would hit the pulley when the sash is pulled to the top and the window would not shut properly.

Then repeat the process on the other side.

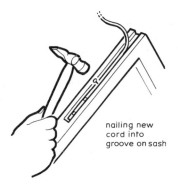

nailing new
cord into
groove on sash

Put the sash into position in the window frame and then take out the tacks you have used to hold the weights at the top of the frame. Run the sash up and down once or twice to see that everything is working as it should.

When you have put the outer sash in place, put back the weight-box covers, then fix back the beads which separate the sashes, using panel pins, starting at the bottom of the frame.

Then attach the cords to the inner sash and put it back. Finally replace the beading at the room side of the window.

Getting unstuck

The 'superglue' adhesives – made from cyanoacrylate – can bond skin as quickly and strongly as they bond the other materials they are designed to stick. A report in *Handyman Which?* in May 1981 advises that 'If this happens to you, never try to pull the stuck areas apart, but soak them in warm soapy water, then gently and slowly peel the affected areas apart using a blunt edge – for example, a teaspoon handle. If lips get stuck together, apply lots of warm water and peel or roll them apart – never pull directly' and recommends getting medical help if in difficulty – go to a hospital accident department if there is one near. There are freeing solvents now available with these adhesives to release any stuck area, but these should not be used on sensitive areas, such as eyes. If adhesive gets into your eyes, *Handyman Which?* says 'Do not panic: seek medical advice. You may experience double vision and a lot of eye-watering but, even in the worst of cases, the glue should come out within a matter of hours – the main danger is of injuring yourself trying to free whatever is stuck.'

If a person gets jammed in an inextricable position, such as head or limb trapped between bars, child stuck on ledge or on branch of a tree, call the fire brigade (not necessarily through the '999' emergency service, unless the person is in imminent danger of falling or otherwise being injured further). Tell them what has happened and where the person is; they will come with appropriate cutting equipment and ladders.

To rescue a cat that has 'treed' itself or any animal that has got stuck – in a pipe or in sludge, for instance – contact the nearest branch of the Royal Society for the Prevention of Cruelty to Animals (find the number in the local telephone directory or through the main RSPCA office at The Causeway, Horsham, Sussex RH12 1HG; telephone Horsham 64181). Someone will come to give advice and help with getting the animal out or down.

trapped bird

Where a bird has fallen down inside the chimney stack, particularly if the fireplace(s) below have now been sealed up, it is a job for a builder to get through the brickwork and plaster to extricate the prisoner. (If it is already too late, and the bird has died, you may just have to leave the body to decompose undisturbed.) It is advisable to put wire netting or a wire ball or cage over the top of a chimney whether the fireplace is used or not.

Often, the fireplace has not been bricked up but simply blocked off with a sheet of plywood, plaster board or similar; if a gas fire has been installed, the gas fitter will have sealed the opening with sheet metal, leaving a small opening for the flue. These removable sheets can be lifted out to free the bird. Do this in daylight, but keep the room in darkness by drawing the curtains across the windows except for one large window or door to the outside. Open this window or door wide and the bird will fly straight to the light and away. Do not try catching a sooty frightened bird who will leave a trail of dirt all over your furnishings.

stuck jar or bottle

When a screw-topped jar is stubborn about opening, put a broad rubber band around the edge of the lid to give a better grip. Try striking down on the edge with the back of a knife or wooden spoon, going all round the lid once or twice. Then try screwing off the lid in the usual way.

A screw-topped bottle can be effectively clamped by using as a vice the gap between the edge of a door and the jamb to which it is hinged. Open the door, trap the cap fairly gently between the door edge and the jamb by partially bringing the door to and gradually tightening the grip of the door edge until it stops the cap from turning; then turn the bottle anti-clockwise. Steadily increase the strength of twist on the bottle until the stuck thread yields. The power exerted by the leverage of the door is considerable, so proceed gently–gently rather than with vigour.

When a stopper gets stuck in the neck of a decanter or other glass container, do not try to exert too much force to get it out – you will probably just break the neck of the decanter. Put the decanter into the refrigerator or deep freeze cabinet to chill the glass down below room temperature. Then hold the neck of the decanter under the hot water tap, turn this on from cold and let it run over the neck part without wetting the stopper while it gradually warms up. (Sudden contact with already hot water could create stress in the glass and crack it.) When the neck part is warm but the stopper still cool, give a quick firm upward twist of the stopper to pull it out (do not try leverage). You may need to do this a few times before it works.

When a vacuum flask has been left closed after being insufficiently washed out, it will develop a tainted smell. This can be dispelled by putting a dessertspoon of salt into the flask and then filling it to the brim with boiling water. Put the cap on but do not screw it down, and leave overnight. Give the flask a good rinse out the next day.

stuck hinge or screw

For a rusted hinge, use a special highly penetrative oil – better for this purpose than ordinary penetrating oil. Leave for a day or two, then squirt on some more oil and try to move the hinge a little. (Put newspaper or an old cloth on the floor below the hinge to catch any drips.) Once you have persuaded the hinge to move just a little, continue to apply copious amounts of oil, while ever increasing the movement until you can get the hinge fully open. Continue lubricating with ordinary penetrating oil while operating the hinge over its full travel several times; leave for a day, then repeat the process.

A stuck window hinge may be released by expanding the straps or holders that go round the pin of the hinge, so that their grip on the pin is loosened. One way is get a big, heavy screwdriver or similar handled piece of metal, heat the end of it in a gas jet or other flame to get it red hot, then bring it to the hinge and hold the red hot end hard against each strap of the hinge in turn (you may be able to do a couple of straps per trip). Conductivity will convey the expanding heat and also sweat free any accumulated paint. Ease the hinge gently to and fro before the metal cools.

Similarly, conductivity can be used where a screw is stuck. Press the heated blade of a large heavy screwdriver into the notch in the screw head and hold it there for about a minute. Heat transfer will sweat the screw head free of paint and expand the shank of the screw. Fractionally turn the screw onwards (clockwise), just a degree or two, and then unscrew (anti-clockwise) normally. Even a stubborn screw will yield to this treatment.

When it is the lock of the door that has stuck, you will have to get a locksmith to release or remove it for you, unless you are prepared to break the lock and/or the door by brute force.

stuck knob on central heating radiator

This may be due to long-term corrosion and accumulated paint. It can also be caused by the valve having been turned down too tightly when very hot and the contraction of the metal on cooling having tightened the grip between the metal screw threads. Excess paint can be gently chipped off with the chisel edge of a hammer. A smear of paint stripper can be used to attack hardened paint. Wear rubber gloves, and work carefully following the instructions and applying a little at a time, using something fairly long-handled.

If the knob is made of any plastic material, take this off first so that leverage is put directly on to the shank peg. Use a stillson-type spanner, but remember that the leverage is very powerful so, if possible, use a second tool to take the strain on the static part. A smart tap or two with a hammer on the extremity of the spanner makes a better start than trying to overcome resistance by sheer strength of arm. If you want to undo a shut valve, turn anti-clockwise; to shut down an open valve, turn clockwise. If time and quick action are not important, a drop or two of easing oil allowed to penetrate may help considerably.

If the stuck part is the venting plug, get the correct sized 'key'. An oversized key or using pliers may chew up the profile of the head of the plug. Keys are available from hardware shops or plumbers' suppliers. If you are in doubt about the correct size, make a mould to take with you: plasticine, soap, pastry dough, a raw potato can be used to take an impression of the plug.

If the plug is stuck because of accumulated paint, use paint stripper to soften it. If the key can get a purchase on the shank of the plug, it can be shocked free by clamping the key in the jaws of an adjustable spanner, holding the key well on to the plug, and giving a smart firm tap, anti-clockwise, on the end of the handle. The aim is to free the thread by breaking the adhesion (it needs only a small movement to do this, so there is no need to give a pile-driving clout with the hammer). The plug should then be movable by finger and thumb on the key. Release the plug gently and slowly. The radiator should fizz air without the plug being wholly removed. Turn it back in again as soon as liquid starts to arrive. The water will be filthy, so hold a piece of towelling or cloth near to guard the wall and floor coverings.

Pests

There are many brands of household insecticide or rodenticide powders and liquids. All chemicals used to kill or control pests must by their nature have some hazard associated with their use: if absolutely safe, they would probably not work. They should be stored away from children and pets and used in accordance with the instructions.

At the first sign of pests you cannot deal with yourself, call in outside help: the quicker they can get to grips with the problem, the easier it is to deal with it and the less damage will be done. A professional pest control company will usually provide treatment at 24 hours' notice.

The British Pest Control Association (telephone 01-582 8268) can let you have a list of member firms in your area who specialise in pest control. The Association's booklet *An A-Z of Household Pests* (60p) gives details of a variety of household pests and how to cope with them.

Nearly all local authorities will deal with rats and mice free, or for a nominal charge. Many local authorities will also provide advice or treatment to get rid of pests such as ants, cockroaches, fleas, lice. They have a duty under the Prevention of Damage by Pests Act to 'take such steps as may be necessary to secure so far as practicable that their district is kept free from rats and mice'. The occupier of any premises has to notify the local authority if there are substantial numbers of rats or mice on his property.

Local authorities are also empowered to deal with pigeons and with insect pests that constitute a public health hazard.

mice

Mice are agile creatures, capable of passing through narrow chinks, and are opportunists in taking advantage of quiet and darkness to find their way inside.

You can tell that you have mice by mice droppings (small dark $\frac{1}{8}$-inch pellets) and gnaw signs not only on food but paper, wood, plastic, even electric cables.

Fill in any spaces, however small – behind battens, edges of wallpaper, skirting board, and where the gas pipes and electric cables emerge. Close off any holes, using wire wool embedded in a crack-filler or epoxy resin. But do not block up air bricks or similar ventilation.

These precautions may help to keep out new mice but the resident generation has to be killed.

Set a number of the spring 'back breaker' type of trap close to each other along known mouse-routes, at right angles to the wall. An habitual route is likely to be seen by a greasy greyish shadowy line, possibly with a few hairs adhering. Do not set the holding bar of a trap so finely that it will go off prematurely nor so far back towards the hinge that it will need more than the weight and movement of the quarry to release the spring. A self-setting metal trap is easier to use and more efficient than the cheaper wooden type trap. Rather than the traditional cheese for bait, use chocolate, dried fruit, nuts, lard.

Do not set traps without warning the rest of the household that you have done so, and try to keep pets and children away. After use, douse a trap with boiling water before setting it again.

Instead of setting traps, you can now buy ready-to-use poison bait (safe, provided it is used in accordance with directions) which causes the mice to die quickly and close to the bait so that the bodies can be easily collected.

If you cannot burn or bury a dead mouse, seal it in a plastic bag before throwing it into the dustbin.

Having a cat is a good antidote to mice.

rats

If you find you have rats, call in the local authority's rodent officer. He is usually attached to the environmental health department.

Tell the rodent officer if you or your neighbours have any pets or free-ranging livestock; if he lays down bait outside the house, it would be a proper courtesy to warn your neighbours.

Ask the rodent officer to write down his recommendations and instructions for you, so that you can refer to them and also pass them on to others, where necessary, without omission or mistake. The officer will return at some later stage to check the efficacy of his efforts and to clear away any of his baits or impedimenta. Make a note of how to contact him in case more rats appear.

ants

Ants are more then casual scavengers. They are organised, resourceful searchers prepared to forage over long distances.

When, after an initial period of scattered and apparently random exploration, ants have successfully located a source of food, they show a behaviour pattern in taking supplies away to their living quarters, moving to and fro along an established trail and keeping to it even if a short cut seems obvious. It is likely to be more successful when dealing with a procession of ants not to scatter the column but to put down plenty of insecticide powder, specific to ants, at the point where they are coming in and out, for them to take down into their quarters.

Liquid or gel baits containing boric acid can be used, which the foraging workers take back to the nest, however inaccessible it may be. Insecticidal lacquer can be sprayed around thresholds, skirtings and points of entry.

If you can trace the ants' nest outside (often between paving slabs), try the old-fashioned remedy of pouring a kettle or two of boiling water between the cracks. This will not reach the queen, so follow it up a few days later with a puffer pack of ant-killer powder.

wasps

You can take advantage of wasps' liking for sweet fruit by making a trap containing a syrup. Stir about 1 teaspoonful of strawberry or other jam into a clear jam jar half-filled with warm water. Put the lid on the jar and give a good shaking to get the sweet mixture frothed up on the inside of the jar. Then punch a funnel-shaped hole downwards into the centre of the lid to make an entrance for the wasps, and stand the trap in a position accessible to them.

A less sadistic way would be to kill individual wasps with an aerosol insecticide.

wasps' nest
If you can trace the wasps' nest, choose a time for dealing with it when the wasps are less active (in the evening when most of them will be at home) and puff into the nest a liberal amount of a proprietary wasps' nest killer. Wear protective clothes and thick gloves.

The insecticide should be effective within a couple of days.

When there is no sign of life, the nest can be dug out (if it is in a bank in the garden) or cut clear with a sharp knife from a wall.

Try to get the whole construction away in one piece if possible, slitting all round the periphery before lifting or pulling it off, in order to avoid spilling the insects. Drop it into a polythene bag and burn it.

Masonry wasps do not live in colonies but prefer a solitary existence, making their own individual burrows in sand. In urban areas, the wasps attack brick or stone walls as a substitute for sand. The brick or stone is not their target: they mine into the soft mortar inbetween and, if not prevented, they can in time seriously damage the walls of a house. So, if you see wasps going into or emerging from holes or cracks in brickwork, prompt action is necessary: squirt insecticide into every hole and spray the surface of the wall. The affected area or, preferably, the whole of that wall should be re-pointed as soon as possible. In normal re-pointing work, the joints are usually raked out to a depth of about half an inch, but where wasps have intruded, a deeper excavation (about 1 inch) is advisable. The re-pointing job should be carried out by a skilled person.

Stains

The important thing is prompt action, particularly with fabrics or anything which is absorbent: try to avoid allowing the spot to dry in. But although quick action is needed, too vigorous an attack is likely to damage the material and leave a permanent mark.

- identify the material or fibre(s) from which the stained fabric is made (you may find this on a sewn-in label)

- try to identify the nature of the substance causing the stain

- apply any liquid for removing the stain cautiously and to the smallest possible area; start with a very small amount, increase the quantity gradually; keep the temperature as low as possible

- treat any chemical, liquid or solid, with great care.

Delicate fabrics, suede, fur, non-washable upholstery and expensive articles may be better dealt with by a professional cleaner. You should report as precisely as possible what caused the stain and, if you have tackled it yourself, jot down on a piece of paper what you used and in what sequence. When you take the article to the dry cleaning shop, attach the written note to the stained area. If the staining substance came out of a tin, bottle or tube, it may be worth also taking the label, or the container itself, with you. For example, tomato-based products, mustards and mayonnaises are made up in various solutions and a professional cleaner may have contacts with the appropriate manufacturing trade about specific antidotes.

getting it off

First try to get off as much as possible of whatever has spilt or dropped before tackling the mark. Act quickly.

If liquid, mop it up. If it is something that solidifies, such as grease, wax or paint, first try to spoon or scrape it up, using a blunt-edged implement or a stiff card (old credit card, perhaps) to lift the substance off the surface. Work inwards from the edges, to avoid spreading the mark.

Any stain is more difficult to eliminate if it is not dealt with immediately. Many stains while fresh can be extracted by means of common liquids such as water or mild bleaching agents such as dilute hydrogen peroxide.

Where a liquid has sunk into a surface, blot with an absorbent pad, such as a cotton rag or piece of towelling, to draw out the liquid; then dilute to neutralize or weaken its strength. Repeat blotting.

Where a spill has in part sunk in so that there is both penetration of the surface and a deposit on top, first take the top layer off and then deal with the absorbed stain.

Where a stain has dried and set, you have to work to reverse what has happened. First, soften the stain. Start gently with a mild preparation (glycerine, for example). If you have softened the stain and the substance is loosened, proceed as for a freshly-made stain. If it will not respond, take it to a professional cleaner. But bear in mind that some stains are not removable – for example, dried emulsion paint.

if washable

After removing as much as possible of the spillage, rinse the stained area in cold water (but not if the stain is tar, varnish, or an oil-based paint because water will 'fix' the stain).

The water must be clean and should be changed frequently. Do not use hot or boiling water unless recommended specifically: cold or lukewarm water is safer and less likely to set the stain.

After rinsing, soak the article in cold water until it can be washed. But wool, silk and flame-resistant treated fabrics may be spoiled by over-soaking, and carpets and upholstery ought not to be left wet.

Hand-launder a washable fabric gently in lukewarm (not hot) suds of an ordinary detergent solution and rinse well, perhaps adding some hydrogen peroxide to the rinsing water for white articles. If possible, dry in sunlight to help take out residual traces of the stain. Do not dry in strong direct heat nor iron over a residual stain: heat will set it.

If the stain is greasy or fatty or the article is not washable or the stain has not been removed by washing, use a stain-removing solvent.

basic rules when using solvent cleaners

- follow the instructions on the container exactly
- use a solvent outdoors or in a well-ventilated room
- do not inhale the vapour
- never use near a naked flame or radiant elements
- do not smoke when using a solvent
- test colour fastness on an inconspicuous part of the fabric before starting treatment (fabrics which are colour fast to one solvent may not be fast to another, so test each one before use)
- do not use on damp or wet fabrics
- hang treated fabric up in the open air if possible afterwards to allow residual solvent to evaporate freely.

Place the front of the stain down on a piece of clean absorbent cloth, such as an old towel. Work on the stain from the back of the fabric, applying the solvent with a cloth or cotton wool. As soon as the cloth underneath becomes stained, move the article to a clean portion, otherwise the stain may re-deposit itself.

Always tackle the stain from its outer edges and work inwards towards the centre. This will prevent the stain from spreading out and leaving a ring mark which, on drying, may be permanent.

If you have treated the fabric with solvent only, it should not be rinsed: the solvent should be removed by thorough airing. If, however, the fabric has previously been washed with detergent or any water-based agent such as peroxide, the area that has been treated with solvent – and preferably the whole article – must be rinsed.

Most solvents are toxic. Keep them well out of the reach of children and of elderly people and anyone with poor vision or impaired sense of smell.

The danger of poisoning is not confined to swallowing the stuff. The fumes are dangerous and can be deadly, so work out of doors if possible, or in a well-ventilated space.

Many solvents are flammable, so do not use a stain remover anywhere near a flame or a radiant heater. A pilot light, even yards away, is enough to ignite an explosion, so turn it off until you have finished working and the air has cleared. Do not smoke; the toxicity of a vapour is more serious when inhaled through a lighted cigarette (or pipe or cigar) and a filter tip is no protection.

Be careful not to get any solvent into or near your eyes.

Preferably wear rubber gloves. All solvents tend to dissolve oils and fats, including those in your skin, so try to keep them off your skin. After working with a solvent, wash your hands and apply a hand cream.

Children should not be allowed near while the cleaning job is in progress; pets also should be kept away (cage birds are especially vulnerable).

on carpets and upholstery
Attend to a spilled liquid straightaway. A quick sharp jet from a soda siphon will help. Blot, blot, blot again and again with clean tissue, towelling or cotton wool (but do not bring the kitchen dishcloth into the action, thereby adding grease to the problem). Do not let the carpet or fabric become wetted more than a moist-to-damp degree: mop up with an old (clean) towel as you work. Avoid rubbing or excessive pressure; this tends to make the stain sink into the pile and increase the difficulties of removing.

Treat the back as well, if you can get at it, but a carpet must be thoroughly dry before re-laying. Be very sparing with any solvent if it is a fitted carpet or there is a foam or rubber backing.

Treat the area afterwards with a carpet shampoo. Do not be tempted to increase the strength of the shampoo dilution beyond the manufacturer's recommendations: you should follow these precisely.

When dried, if a lightened patch there reveals how grubby the rest of the carpet has become, take this as a hint to shampoo the whole carpet as soon as convenient.

Where milk or a milky beverage was spilt, although you may be able to remove the stain, a smell may develop. So, if more than a little was spilt, the sooner the carpet is professionally cleaned, the better.

With upholstery, it is also important to act quickly, and keep on blotting up with something clean as you work. Acrylic pile can be sponged clean with a warm cloth dosed with a little enzyme detergent solution and well wrung out. Do not wet through to the backing into which the pile is woven, otherwise it will lose shape and develop cockled ridges which will not disappear on drying.

Velvets and brocades should be treated by a professional, preferably in situ. When making the arrangements for the specialist cleaner to come, tell him as much as you can about the fabric and the stain and what you have done about it, if anything.

making up a cleaning kit

It is worth assembling a collection of removing agents so that you have the proper cleaner readily available.

There are pre-packed cleaning kits on the market containing a selection of removers for different purposes, labelled and with instructions, fitted into a special container. A kit has the advantage of easy storage and accessibility, but they are relatively expensive.

A wide range of proprietary cleaning preparations is obtainable at chemists and hardware shops, some to deal with more than one contingency, others for specialised use, such as for urine, chewing gum, ink marks, adhesives.

There are a number of proprietary stain removers, all solvents, for dealing with greasy stains. The brand names of stain removing agents and dry cleaning fluids do not always make it possible or easy to recognise the chemical ingredient. With man-made fibres and more sophisticated cleaning agents, it is necessary to be careful not to put incompatibles together. The manufacturers' instructions should be followed precisely.

Also, there are household preparations such as detergents, methylated spirit, ammonia, and chemicals such as lighter fuel, which, although not specifically for stain removing, can be efficacious in getting rid of stains or helping to reduce their effect.

Have nothing anonymous: keep a label on the container and see that it does not come off during use or storage. Do not swap liquids from one bottle into another: a swig taken from a lemonade bottle containing a corrosive liquid could be fatal.

cleaning agents and their uses

acetone
useful for unsticking misplaced adhesive
highly flammable; do not inhale

can be bought at chemists as non-oily nail varnish remover

DO NOT USE ON acetate, triacetate

ammonia
a neutralizer: use where mark has been made by an acid
should be diluted: 1 tablespoon to 3 tablespoons water
test for colour fastness before using on coloured fabrics: colour may 'bleed'
a few drops can be added to rinsing water or to bleach solution (1 teaspoon
    to 3 pints) for coloureds
gives off fumes; keep away from eyes, and off skin and clothing

buy as cloudy household ammonia

DO NOT USE ON wool, silk

amyl acetate
has similar solvent properties as acetone when used for removing stains but
    can be used on acetate and triacetate fabrics

do not inhale

can be bought as moisturised or oily nail varnish remover

bleach
does not really remove stains but destroys the colouring matter causing them
must be diluted according to manufacturer's instructions
test for colour fastness before using on coloured fabrics, and do not soak
    coloureds for more than about half an hour; whites can stand longer

various proprietary household brands available

DO NOT USE ON drip-dry fabrics, crease-resistant fabrics, embossed or
    piqué fabrics, silk or woollen materials

borax
has a bleaching, alkaline effect
for soaking, use a solution of 1 tablespoon in about ¾ pint warm water
safe for most fabrics, but do not soak for more than ¼ hour
sponge with it if soaking unsuitable
with white fabrics, stretch material horizontally over sink or basin, moisten
    the stain, sprinkle borax over it and then slowly pour hot water through the
    mark until it has gone

can be bought in powder form as laundry or domestic borax

---

carbon tetrachloride
for grease-based stains
toxic fumes: do not inhale and do not smoke while using

can be bought as dry cleaning fluid

DO NOT USE ON acetate, triacetate, plastics

---

enzyme detergents
for animal-derived protein stains, such as blood, egg, milk, sweat
should be thoroughly dissolved, following manufacturer's instructions about
    strength, pre-soaking and rinsing
test for colour fastness before using on coloured fabrics

various proprietary brands available; often called 'biological' washing powder

DO NOT USE ON wool, silk, crease-resistant fabrics, flame-resistant fabrics,
    rubberised fabrics

---

french chalk, fuller's earth
absorbs liquid and grease (talcum powder can be used to same effect)

can be bought at chemists as prepared powder

---

glycerine
for softening stains as prelude to removal treatment
apply in a dilution of equal quantities glycerine and warm water (do not add
    anything else to the water); rub in and leave for about an hour before rinsing
    or sponging out

can be bought as clear viscous liquid

---

hot iron
to melt wax: place piece of absorbent paper or cloth over (and, where possible,
    under) wax mark, and apply iron

DO NOT USE ON man-made fibres, foam-filled upholstery

hydrogen peroxide
acts as a bleach, by oxidation
dilute with 6 times the amount of water to peroxide
for coloureds, add a teaspoon of ammonia (unless there is any wool content
    in the fabric) to each couple of litres of peroxide and water solution to speed
    up bleaching action so that fabric can be soaked for shorter period

buy in 20 vol strength; keep in dark-coloured glass bottle to prevent decom-
    position by light

DO NOT USE ON nylon, flame-resistant fabrics

lemon juice (citric acid)
can be used on rust marks, iron mould, old ink stains

liquid lighter fuel
for grease-based stains
highly flammable; do not inhale

DO NOT USE ON acetate, triacetate

methylated spirit
apply neat, then blot with clean absorbent paper or cloth
test for colour fastness before using on coloured fabrics
highly flammable and poisonous; noxious odour (persisting)

can be bought in hardware shops and chemists

DO NOT USE ON acetate, triacetate

salt
sprinkle or pour on to absorb and prevent spilled liquid spreading
particularly useful for blood, wine, fruit juice, beetroot spills
may not be easy to extract from pile carpet and may affect colour

stain removers
solvents useful for grease-based stains
follow manufacturer's instructions precisely
some are flammable
do not inhale or use in confined space
keep off skin

various proprietary brands; some aerosols

DO NOT USE ON acetate, triacetate, plastics, leather

surgical spirit
similar properties as methylated spirit when used as stain remover

can be bought at chemists

---

turpentine substitute
see white spirit

---

water
sponge, rinse or soak stain as soon as possible in cold water (hot water will set some stains)
quick squirt from a soda siphon useful when stain on carpet or upholstery (particularly beer, blood, wine)
use with detergent as part of stain-removing treatments

DO NOT USE ON non-washable fabrics, electric blankets (unless 'washable')

---

white spirit
for grease-based stains, tar, oil-based paint, polish
flammable; do not inhale

can be bought in hardware shops; also as paint thinner

DO NOT USE ON acetate, triacetate

---

white vinegar (acetic acid)
for sponging off marks from non-washables
do not leave in contact for long; test for colour fastness before using on coloured fabrics
can be used in lieu of carpet shampoo for water-based stains: make up solution with 1 teaspoon white vinegar and 1 teaspoon detergent to 1 litre of warm water

DO NOT USE ON acetate, triacetate

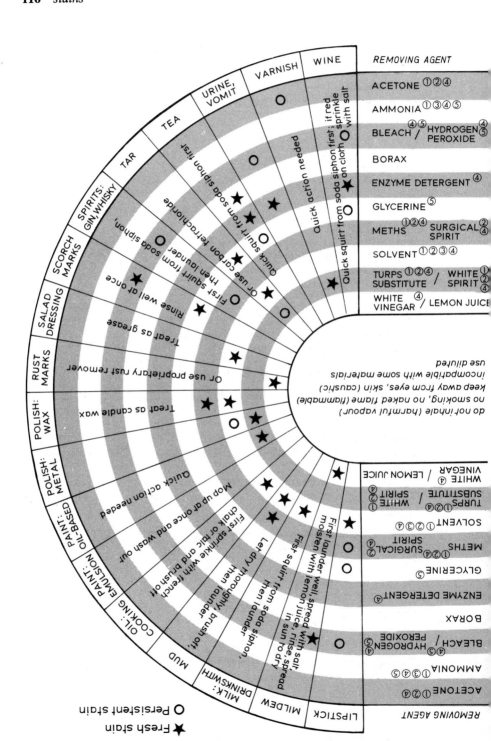

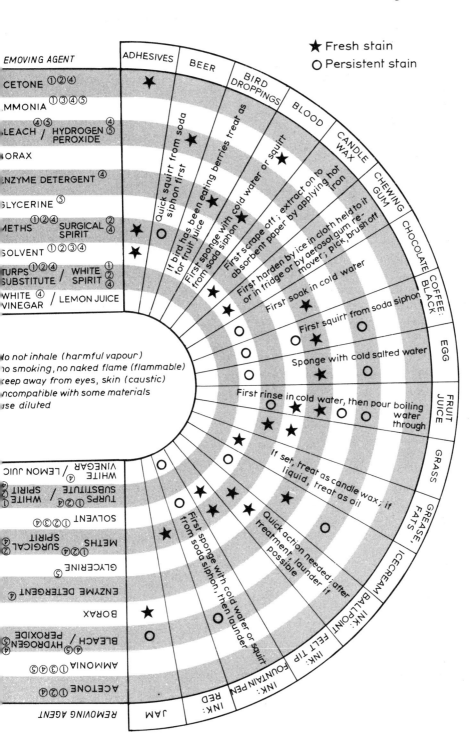

★ Fresh stain
O Persistent stain

REMOVING AGENT

ACETONE ①②④
AMMONIA ①③④⑤
BLEACH ④⑤ / HYDROGEN ④⑤ PEROXIDE
BORAX
ENZYME DETERGENT ④
GLYCERINE ⑤
METHS ①②④ SURGICAL ②④ SPIRIT
SOLVENT ①②③④
TURPS ①②④ / WHITE ① SUBSTITUTE ② SPIRIT ④
WHITE ④ / LEMON JUICE VINEGAR

No do not inhale (harmful vapour)
no smoking, no naked flame (flammable)
keep away from eyes, skin (caustic)
incompatible with some materials
use diluted

ADHESIVES
BEER
BIRD DROPPINGS
BLOOD
CANDLE WAX
CHEWING GUM
CHOCOLATE
COFFEE: BLACK
EGG
FRUIT JUICE
GRASS
GREASE, FATS
ICECREAM
INK: BALLPOINT
INK: FELT TIP
INK: FOUNTAIN PEN
INK: RED
JAM

Quick squirt from soda siphon first

If bird has been eating berries treat as for fruit juice

First sponge with cold water or squirt from soda siphon

First scrape off; extract on to absorbent paper by applying hot iron

First harden by ice in cloth held to it or in fridge or by aerosol gum remover; pick, brush off

First soak in cold water

First squirt from soda siphon

Sponge with cold salted water

First rinse in cold water, then pour boiling water through

If set, treat as candle wax; if liquid, treat as oil

Quick action needed; after treatment, launder it possible

First sponge with cold water or squirt from soda siphon, then launder

REMOVING AGENT
WHITE / LEMON JUICE VINEGAR
TURPS ①②④ / WHITE SUBSTITUTE SPIRIT
SOLVENT ①②③④
METHS ①②④ SURGICAL SPIRIT ②④
GLYCERINE ⑤
ENZYME DETERGENT ④
BORAX
BLEACH ④⑤ / HYDROGEN ④⑤ PEROXIDE
AMMONIA ①③④⑤
ACETONE ①②④

Immediate first aid after an accident

Keep first aid equipment in a metal or plastic box, clearly labelled. If all first aid equipment is kept together in a box, it is easy to get someone to bring the whole box to you, rather than have to make several trips to find each item as you want it. Keep it in a cupboard easily accessible to adults at all times, but difficult for a small child to reach and to open.

suggested contents of emergency first aid box
1 pack of small paper tissues
2 small packs of cotton wool
2 white bandages, 5cm wide
1 white crepe bandage, 7½cm wide
1 triangular bandage
2 PFA (perforated film absorbent) dressings 10 × 10cm
1 PFA dressing 10 × 20cm (PFA dressings are individually packed sterile
   dressings; the shiny side goes on the wound)
2 large, 2 medium plain wound dressings
(individually packed combinations of sterile dressing, pad and bandage)
adhesive dressing strip, 2½cm wide (small pieces as needed can be cut
   from it)
1 packet plain white gauze
pair of scissors
pair of tweezers
safety pins
large clean handkerchief, folded
antihistamine cream
As soon as anything has been used, replace it with a new supply.

calling medical help

- call ambulance
- call your GP
- call any trained first-aider
- go to hospital accident/emergency department
- go to your GP's next 'surgery'

Do not hesitate about calling medical help when indicated.

In a case of an emergency such as choking, poisoning, severe burns, heavy bleeding, unconsciousness, it is wiser to call an ambulance, on the emergency 999 number, rather than lose time trying to get your general practitioner. The doctor may be out on his rounds or not able to come at once.

The ambulance service does not usually come to a case of illness without a doctor's request, but will come to a genuine accident at anyone's call. Diall '999' and when the operator answers, ask for 'ambulance'.

For less immediate cases, when the victim's condition is not so critical, it is sensible to contact the general practitioner.

The message must give very clearly

- the name and address
- the nature of the injury and degree of urgency
- any special circumstances.

Do not, however, rush away from the victim to call for help as soon as the accident has happened. Give immediate help and first aid. Then, if you can, stay with the victim and use a messenger to call medical help. Write down on a piece of paper exactly what you want him or her to say and whom to call.

If your house is not particularly easy to find, let the messenger or someone else, after telephoning, stand in a strategic place to guide the arriving doctor or ambulance. At night (when house numbers cannot easily be read), have the front room and hall lights on, the curtains drawn back and the door open as a guiding beacon. Let the doctor or ambulance service know you are doing this.

first aid

First aid not only involves knowing what to do but also what not to do:

DO NOT give alcohol in any form

DO NOT give food or fluids to a drowsy or unconscious person who cannot swallow (risk of choking) or to someone likely to need an anaesthetic

DO NOT move a person who may have a fracture until the injured part has been properly immobilised or protected – in particular, never move someone who may have injured his spine

DO NOT leave an unconscious person on his back (unless he must not be moved because of the possibility of fracture)

DO NOT use a tourniquet as a way of controlling bleeding.

---

artificial respiration (when breathing has stopped)

If breathing has stopped, immediately

- get the victim on his back
- scoop out any obstruction (vomit, denture, mud) from his mouth with your finger
- bend his head well backwards with the palm of your hand on his forehead
- pinch the nose shut with the thumb and forefinger of the same hand
- keep the jaw pushed forward and the mouth open with your other hand (be careful that your thumb and fingers stay clear of the lips and the edge of your hand does not press on the throat)
- take in a good breath
- open your mouth wide and seal your lips firmly round the victim's mouth
  (with a small child, do not pinch his nose but seal your mouth around his nose and mouth)
- breathe out from your lungs into the victim's mouth and so into his lungs
  do this firmly with no more force than is needed to make his chest rise (particularly important with a small child)

begin with four quick breaths
then proceed with slower, normal breathing
- after each breath has gone in, take your mouth off and turn your head sideways to look at the person's chest to confirm whether it has risen
breathe in to fill your lungs again while you watch his chest fall, expelling its air
- as soon as his chest has fallen, again apply your mouth around the victim's open mouth and breathe into it

you will find that this sequence takes about 5 seconds for an adult and a little less for a small child

- continue without stopping until medical or other help arrives and takes over.

If you are successful, the victim will after a time begin breathing for himself, although weakly. If he vomits, quickly turn his head to one side and clear his mouth.

Place him in the recovery position and stay by him. Watch lest again he cease to breathe.

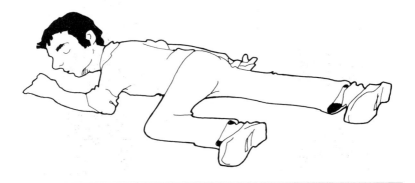

bitten by dog or cat

Treat as wound.

The risk of tetanus (lockjaw) is relatively high, even if the wound is only a small puncture. Go to your GP or the nearest hospital accident department. Even when the victim has already been immunised against tetanus, the doctor may give a reinforcing injection of tetanus toxoid, and perhaps prescribe an antibiotic as well.

bleeding from a wound

Mild bleeding can be controlled by a firmly applied dressing. ('Dressing' is a general term for anything appropriate – from a clean handkerchief to special sterile gauze.)

For severe bleeding, immediately

- press the edges of the wound together very firmly with fingers and thumb, or press the palm of your hand over the wound
  maintain this pressure without interruption for at least 10 minutes
- lay the victim down and, if possible, raise the bleeding part (leg, arm) unless a fracture is suspected

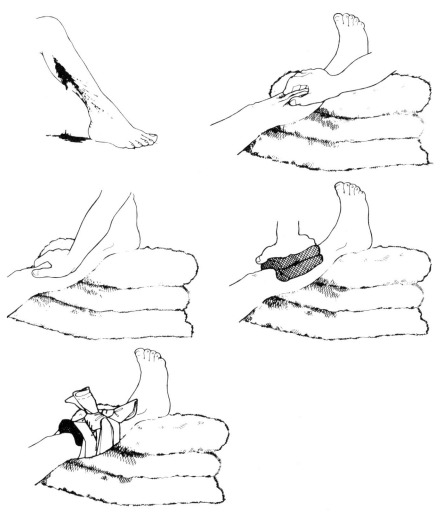

- slip a thick pad (folded handkerchief, towel, cotton wool) under your hand, then knot a firm bandage (belt, necktie, stocking, scarf will do) over the pad, to replace the hand's pressure
- watch the site: if blood still seeps out, add another pad and bandage it firmly over the first one
- take action to minimise shock

DO NOT apply a tourniquet: it is both inefficient and harmful.

burnt or scalded

Cool the burnt or scalded part with cold water, for about 10 minutes. If it is a finger tip, hold it under running water; if a hand, arm, foot or leg, immerse in a bucket or sink. If other parts, cover well with a pad or thick cloth saturated with cold water applied flat over the burnt area, if possible; as pad loses coolness, keep renewing it.

Maintain this cooling for at least 10 minutes; longer if the pain is not considerably relieved.

There is no need to use ice: ordinary cold water works better; do not use jet of shower or hose; do not plunge the victim into a cold bath: this would be excessive.

Remove any tight objects (rings, bracelets, wristwatch, garters) from the burnt part if possible, because swelling may develop. Keep burnt leg or arm raised.

DO NOT apply creams, lotions or antiseptics
DO NOT burst or prick blisters: they should be left as they are, protected with a loose dressing, such as gauze.
DO NOT put cotton wool directly on to a blister.

Cover the burnt area fully with a clean dry cloth, handkerchief, towel, pillow slip; bandage it on lightly.

Severe burns can be dangerous; call ambulance or doctor unless the burn is slight.

Minimise the effect of shock: if the victim is fully conscious, give half a cupful of tepid water with a pinch of salt and sugar to sip slowly, about every 10 minutes (or tea with sugar).

Scalds in the mouth can cause swelling which may obstruct the airway. If the victim is conscious, given him ice to suck.

burns from chemical
(for example, from strong acids or alkalis, ammonia, bleach)

At once wash away the chemical with a copious flow of water for at least 10 minutes. Take off any contaminated clothing, then treat as for an ordinary burn.

DO NOT attempt to neutralise the substance by applying another chemical.

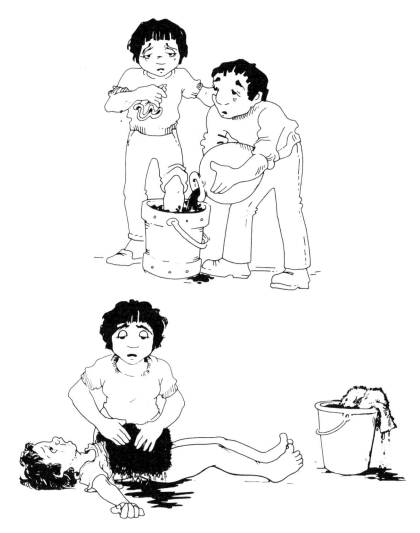

A chemical in the eye needs the same washing out, for about 10 minutes, but do not let the flow of water be forceful. Turn the victim on to the burnt side so that contaminated water does not flow into the other eye. If the eyelids are closed in painful spasm, they have to be gently held open.

Put a dry pad lightly over the eye and get the person to a doctor or hospital.

clothes on fire

Quickly get the victim on to the ground, burning part uppermost. Douse the flames with water, or smother with the nearest available thick material – towel, rug, blanket, coat (but not nylon or similar flammable man-made fibre).

DO NOT try to get burning clothes off; do not remove burnt clothing adhering to the skin.

DO NOT roll victim on the floor: this is liable to increase the burns.

A person on fire who is alone or unhelped should try to grab a rug, tablecloth or any other cloth, and roll in it on the floor.

Then treat the burns.

---

choking (on something swallowed)

If the victim can still breathe and cough, do not interfere beyond standing by and encouraging him to relax and to give big forceful coughs rather than a number of small irregular coughs.

If the victim cannot cough or breathe properly
- bend him over with his head low, your other hand supporting the front of his chest (hold a small child, with head low, over your knee or on your thigh)
  give four hard blows to the back between the shoulder blades with the heel of your hand

● If the back blows fail, at once try an abdominal thrust: stand close behind the victim, encircle his body with your arms, and place the thumb side of one closed fist firmly in the soft area above the navel and below the breastbone.

  Grasp this fist with your other hand, and give a sharp thrust with both hands upwards and into the victim's abdomen.

DO NOT press on the breastbone: your fist should be clearly below its lower end.

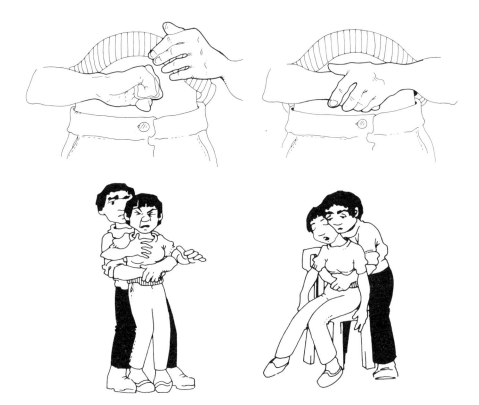

Repeat three or four times, if necessary; each thrust should be separate and distinct.

For a baby, use the index and middle fingers of both hands for the thrusts.

If the victim is on the floor, get him quickly on his back with his head straight. Kneel astride him. Place the heel of one hand in position between the navel and the lower end of the breastbone; put the heel of the other hand over this. Bend forward so that your shoulders are just above your hands and give a thrust this way.

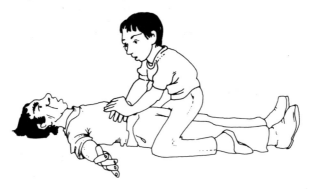

If the object which was caught comes up into the mouth, you must immediately retrieve it (taking care not to push it back again, or to let the person re-inhale it).

If not, keep on alternating three or four back blows with three or four abdominal thrusts. Call an ambulance. If the victim stops breathing, giving artificial respiration may succeed in forcing some air past the obstruction.

Someone choking when alone can try to give himself abdominal thrusts with his own hands, or against a firm object at a suitable height, such as a rail or the back of a chair.

The victim should be checked by a doctor afterwards because the powerful thrusts may have caused internal damage.

coldness

Under abnormally cold circumstances, hypothermia (very low body temperature) can develop even indoors, particularly in a baby or an elderly person. The skin is white (with babies sometimes flushed) and icy cold to the touch, even under bedclothes. The victim is lethargic and unresponsive, or even unconscious. This is an emergency – but must be treated gently.

DO NOT apply a hot water bottle or an electric blanket – too rapid warming could be fatal; the person must warm up slowly
DO NOT place the victim directly in front of a fire or heater
DO NOT give any form of alcohol

- give warm drinks if the victim is conscious
- keep him at rest, warmly, but loosely, covered
- warm up the room around him
- send for medical help.

electric shock

Immediately switch off or disconnect the current.
DO NOT touch the person until this has been done.

If you cannot disconnect the electricity, prise or push or knock the victim away from the cause, using a dry non-conducting material, such as a wooden stick or chair or thickly folded cloth.

If the victim has stopped breathing, give artificial respiration.

Send for medical help.

If there is no heart beat, heart massage should be started after four mouth-to-mouth inflations.

Lay the person on his back on a hard surface.

Kneel beside the body and apply the heel of the right hand over the lower half of his breastbone, and the heel of the left hand across the top of the right hand. Compress the chest firmly, but not violently, at a rate of about 60 times per minute. You can stop intermittently, to feel for the person's pulse in the hope that the procedure will have started the heart beating on its own. If necessary, the procedure should be continued, alternating massage with mouth-to-mouth inflation (for instance, 5 compressions of the chest, one mouth-to-mouth inflation, repeating the sequence) until medical help arrives.

DO NOT give heart massage before giving artificial respiration.

A burn caused by electricity can be widespread in tissues underneath a small burn that shows on the skin. Get medical advice.

eye wound

Cover eye with a large soft pad and get medical help immediately. If possible, get the victim to look downwards and close eyelids before covering with pad. This is the most comfortable position to maintain. If movement of the eye hurts, as when something is embedded, both eyes should be covered because movement of one is accompanied by similar movement of the other. Stay with and reassure the person: a sense of blindness can be panic-making.

fainting

Lay the sufferer down, with legs raised, or sit him down and make him bend his head forward low between his knees. Tell him to breathe slowly. Loosen his clothes.
When he recovers, give him a drink of water.

fracture suspected

If in doubt, treat as a fracture whenever a blow is followed by pain or swelling or the part becoming deformed, bruised, or difficult or impossible to use.

Attend at once to any severe bleeding or wound, but with minimal disturbance.

Tell the victim to stay still and avoid movements of the affected part. Stop others moving him, unless he is in danger where he is.
Make him as comfortable as possible, and protect the injured part from movement by placing against it a rolled-up towel, blanket, pouffe or hard object buffered with cushions or folded cloth.
Get medical help.
Treat to minimise shock.
A fracture of the spine should be suspected whenever someone has fallen from a height or has neck or back pain. Great harm (loss of feeling, paralysis) can be done by movement. Get medical help as quickly as possible, and DO NOT move him.

head injured

Suspect fracture of the skull if there is marked bruising or swelling, bleeding from ear or nose or bruising around the eye. Get medical help. In the meantime, keep the victim at rest. If there is bleeding from the ear, put a light cover over the ear and lie him on that side; do not plug the ear.

If the person loses consciousness, this may be due to concussion (a temporary shaking-up of the brain, causing no permanent damage). Even without loss of consciousness, any symptoms of nausea, increasing headache and depressed consciousness may indicate some brain damage and immediate medical attention is needed.

While the person is dazed or has only just regained consciousness, keep him in the recovery position (in case he vomits) and under observation until medical help arrives.

---

poisoned

If the person is unconscious, check at once whether he is breathing; if not, give artificial respiration.
If the person is conscious, find out what he has taken.
Give him bland drinks (water, milk, barley water) to sip slowly.

DO NOT give salt and water.

Immediately call for an ambulance. Keep the person under close observation until it comes: he may become unconscious; he may stop breathing. Send to the hospital any container(s) of what was swallowed.

In general, DO NOT try to make the person vomit, but if he does so, the contents may help the hospital to identify the poison.

---

shock

Shock can occur after any severe accident, blood loss, injuries such as a large wound, burns or fracture.
A person in a state of shock becomes pale with bluish lips; skin cold and clammy; pulse and breathing weak and rapid.
He is thirsty, mentally vague, restless or comatose or even unconscious.
Do not wait for any of these features to develop before taking measures:
- immediately control any severe bleeding
- minimise movements – the person must be at rest
- lay him down with head low and legs raised about 18 to 24 inches (but DO NOT move limbs if you suspect them to be fractured)

- loosen tight clothing – belt, braces, corset, collar
- keep the person warm with good covering above and, if necessary, also underneath him (but do not lift him if there is any possibility that his spine is damaged)
  DO NOT warm him with hot water bottles
- dress any open wound
- comfort him with reassurance, sympathy and confidence
- if he is thirsty, moisten his lips or give a wet handkerchief to suck
  DO NOT give anything by mouth, such as water, tea (except to victim of burns)
  DO NOT give alcohol.

sprains and strains

Sprains (wrenched ligaments at a joint) and strains (over-stretched and torn muscle fibres) may mimic fractures. If uncertain, treat as a fracture.

If there is no likelihood of fracture, apply a cold compress: soak a cloth in water, wring it out until only just wet, and lay it on the damaged area for about 30 minutes, renewing it as it dries.

Let the victim choose the limb's most comfortable position; support it with firm (not tight) turns of crepe bandage over a layer of cotton wool (but not if there is also a cut or open wound). Warn the person to loosen this if the limb becomes numb or cold.

stung by bee or wasp

Someone with a wasp allergy should be rushed to hospital.
Cool the area with water. Smooth on an antihistamine cream.

If a bee sting has been left in the skin, pull it out with fine tweezers; pull at the sting close to the skin.

If the sting was to mouth or throat, give ice to suck, and get medical help quickly: there is danger of severe swelling obstructing the airway.

unconscious

If the victim is not breathing, give artificial respiration at once.
If the victim is trying to breathe but having difficulty because of a blocked airway, gently but fully bend his head right back by pressing

the chin upwards; this may move the tongue from where it is obstructing the throat. Clear away any foreign matter (vomit, dentures) from the back of the throat.

Then

- control any bleeding
- dress any wounds
- look for evidence of possible fracture (for example, deformity and swelling in a limb)

If you suspect fracture(s) or if the circumstances (for example, found near fallen ladder) suggest back or neck damage, do not move him.

- loosen tight clothing
- if no fracture apparent, turn the victim gently into the recovery position.

Be careful not to make unguarded remarks: the apparently unconscious can often hear and register what is said.

---

wounded

- immediately control any severe bleeding
- lay or sit the victim down
- cover the wound temporarily with something clean while you wash your hands and collect the cleansing materials and dressings you will need
- clean all round the wound (not the wound itself) with soap and water, with straight short strokes, using fresh bits of swab, gauze or clean material for each stroke
- remove from the wound any foreign bodies that can be wiped off easily

DO NOT try to pull out something deeply embedded, nor a splinter that has penetrated deeply

DO NOT disturb any blood clots that have formed at the wound

DO NOT use antiseptic solutions or cream

- cover the wound and the area around it with a clean dressing

A dressing can be improvised from a clean folded towel or handker-

chief: carefully hold it up by two corners, let it fall open and refold it so that the inner surface now becomes the outer one to be applied to the wound. (While refolding, keep it up in the air, handle only the corner tips and keep your hands off the other parts.) Over this, apply a thick pad of gauze, cotton wool, folded handkerchief or towel.
● bandage firmly (but not tightly).

If an object is embedded in the wound, cover it loosely with the dressing; shape another dressing into a raised frame around the embedded object. This keeps off the pressure of the pad and bandage. Get the wound seen to by a nurse or doctor.

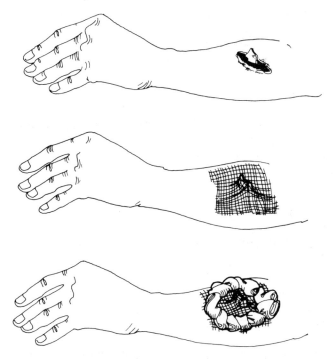

Get medical help for:
a wound in hands or feet which may have injured tendons
a deep or wide wound which may need stitching
a wound contaminated by soil or from an animal bite, which may need an anti-tetanus injection.

abdominal wound

Lay the person on his back, with knees and hips half bent: this relaxes pull on the wound. Loosen tight clothing. Put on a large dressing as for an ordinary wound, but not too tightly.

DO NOT interfere with anything projecting from the tissues, and take care not to push it farther in when applying the dressing.

open wound in the chest

Immediately close it up: press your hand over the wound and keep it there while you get hold of a thick pad (folded cioth, towel, scarf) to replace your hand; bandage firmly to the chest, making as near an air-tight seal as you can. Lay the victim down towards the injured side. If breathing is difficult, half-prop him up on pillows or folded blankets to ease this. Call an ambulance.

learning first aid

In a first aid course, you can learn all procedures for dealing with accidents in the home, including practical exercises; also many other subjects such as the action to take after a car accident or what help to give someone who has an asthmatic, epileptic, cardiac attack. Learning first aid from qualified instructors, with opportunities to practise procedures in a relaxed, friendly atmosphere, should instill the knowledge and confidence which are essential for successfully dealing with an emergency.

Courses are run in most parts of the country during daytime and in the evening by:

The St John Ambulance Association
1 Grosvenor Crescent, London SW1X 7EF

The St Andrew's Ambulance Association
48 Milton Street, Glasgow G4 0HR

The British Red Cross Society
9 Grosvenor Crescent, London SW1X 7EJ

Their local branches are listed in the telephone directory, and can give details of times and charges for courses in your area.

These organisations publish a manual and various booklets about first aid; a list and prices can be obtained from the headquarters.

Claiming on insurance

When some disaster has happened for which you think you are insured, look carefully at any insurance policies you have, including the general conditions section, to check whether this particular circumstance is specifically covered, or appears to be covered by general implication. Even if you are in doubt, claim.

Report the event without delay and say that you want to make a claim. If you delay, the insurers might say that you are in breach of the policy condition requiring full notification as soon as possible.

If the insurers say that the event is excluded from cover, or that you are in breach of a policy condition, it is up to them to show that this is so. Most insurance companies are willing to consider borderline cases if you explain fully what happened.

Once you have informed your insurers of the damage or accident, they will send or give you a claim form to complete. If yours is a Lloyd's insurance policy, you have to ask the broker for a claim form.

Do not delay returning the claim form by waiting, for example, for estimates or bills to substantiate the claim.

Check whether you may go ahead immediately with getting a repair done or whether the insurers require you to get estimates. Keep all bills or receipts, including any for emergency repairs: the insurers will want to see them (you can claim the cost of material, but not the time taken, for d-i-y repairs). Where the insurers pay to replace an article, they can, strictly speaking, take the damaged one, so do not dispose of anything you are claiming for without checking first with them.

A claim for a small amount – perhaps up to £100 – is often settled without further enquiry. Larger amounts involve a varying degree of investigation and negotiation.

The sum for which you are insured should be the full value. If you are under-insured, your claim may be reduced proportionately.

When you claim on a buildings policy for a replacement or repair, the amount you get may be reduced because of 'betterment'. An insured person must not be placed in a position better than he was at the time of the loss or damage. So, the insurers need pay only the proportion of the cost that gets you back to the same state as before, and you have to pay the difference. For instance, if what you had was in a dilapidated state before it was damaged, you may have to pay a contribution towards the improved state it will be in after repair or restoration.

One of the conditions of most householder's policies is that the building will be maintained in good condition, so you will not be paid for breakages or damage arising from neglect or inadequate maintenance.

for broken glass or sanitary fixtures

There is usually cover for accidental damage to fixed glass (windows, skylights, fanlights, glass in doors) and wash basins, sinks, baths, bidets, w.c. pans and cisterns. Cracks can be claimed for as well as complete breakages. If you break a mirror or the plate glass on top of or in a piece of furniture, you can claim on a contents policy but not a buildings policy.

In most cases, it is necessary to get broken glass in windows or doors replaced as soon as possible and to repair broken sanitary ware, such as w.c. cistern, without delay. If this means calling on an emergency service whose charges are high for work done out of normal hours, the insurers should meet these charges in full, but you may need to point out to them that having the work done in this way avoided further damage and saved a larger claim.

for damage from overflowing water

You can claim for damage caused by water overflowing from a water pipe or cistern or any other apparatus capable of holding water – but not for repairing or replacing a tank, cistern, pipe, or other receptacle.

You can also claim on your policy for damage caused by water escaping from a fixed installation on somebody else's property – be it your neighbour's or the water authority's – or from natural flooding.

There are some borderline cases, such as water overflowing into the house from guttering that is blocked or drains that have become obstructed, which insurers may sometimes consider due to failure to maintain the property in a reasonable state of repair. However, do not hesitate to claim and let the insurers decide about the circumstances.

On the overflowing water section of a buildings policy, there is usually an 'excess' (meaning that you do not get paid a set amount of a claim) of, say, £15 or whatever figure was set in the policy; in a contents policy, however, no excess applies.

Where water damage does not cause total destruction of any of your belongings but necessitates cleaning or restoring, you should claim for the cost of this.

Similarly, damage caused by oil leaking from a fixed heating installation can be claimed for on a buildings or a contents policy.

for damage to underground pipes

Accidental damage to underground pipes or cables, such as telephone cables, fuel oil pipes, water and gas pipes, electricity cables, is fully covered by a householder's policy, provided that the damage really was accidental and not due to normal wear and tear. Frost damage to underground water pipes counts as accidental.

for fire damage

Fire damage is covered by a buildings policy and a contents policy, unless the property has been damaged by a fire caused by one of the perils specifically excluded in the conditions of the policy.

The principle of 'proximate cause' applies. This means that if a fire breaks out in your house and you use a mat or coat or other article for smothering it and this gets damaged, the proximate cause of that damage is the fire and you can therefore claim for the mat or coat even though it was not initially part of the fire. Any damage caused to your property by the firemen in the course of putting out the fire can be claimed for on the fire section of a contents policy.

Furniture, even if not actually damaged by flames, may need cleaning and restoration as a result of being drenched with water by the firemen or scorched or damaged by smoke. And if there has been a lot of smoke in the house, your curtains and clothes may need cleaning to get rid of the smell. Claim for the cost of all this. If there is a lot of mess and you have to get in a firm to clear up, the cost of this, too, can be claimed for.

Scorching – that is, damage to woodwork or decorations or clothes due to their being too close to a source of heat within its normal bounds – is not covered by the fire section of a policy unless there was actual ignition. Nevertheless, claims for damage by scorching are sometimes met on an ex gratia basis, so it is always worth including this on a claim.

In the case of a large fire, there is usually a good deal of damage to the building as well as to what is inside it. Claims can be made simultaneously on a buildings and a contents policy – although you will not get paid twice for the same item. The insurers may send a loss adjuster to look at the damage, in order to assess your claim on their behalf.

ombudsman
If you fail to agree about a claim with your insurance company and the company participates in the Insurance Ombudsman Scheme, you can ask the ombudsman to deal with the complaint. Write (within six months of your final failure to agree) with brief details to the Insurance Ombudsman Bureau, 31 Southampton Row, London WC1B 5HJ.

some examples of when and what you can claim on a householder's policy

Notes

current value
present-day price allowing for depreciation, i.e. what it would cost to buy the article in the condition it was in at the time of its destruction or damage

replacement cost
now offered by most companies: what it would cost to buy a new article in replacement of the destroyed one, provided premium paid for this amount (but some exclusions e.g. clothes, household linen)

deduction for betterment
difference between the value of the restored item and value in the condition it was in at the time of the damage

average
if you are under-insured, a claim is proportionately reduced

unoccupancy clause
no cover when the house is not sufficiently furnished for full habitation or is left empty for more than 30 days

excess
the insurance does not pay £xx (usually at least £15) of a claim, nor any claim below that figure

extension
specific addition to the standard policy, for which additional premium paid

the happening	policy cover		what you get
			current market value (or cost of new replacement if insured on this basis) or cost of repairs – but never more than sum insured for which premium paid
fire damages a room and its contents			
decorations ruined, woodwork burned	buildings	fire	cost of repair and redecoration (may be deduction for betterment)
carpets, curtains, furniture burned	contents	fire	cost of repair or current value (or replacement

damage to landlord's fixture and fittings, for which you are liable as tenant	contents	tenant's liability	not more than set percentage (usually 10%) of sum insured, unoccupancy clause applies
clothes soiled or burned, valuables (pictures, jewellery, silver) damaged	contents	fire	not more than set percentage of sum insured for any one article unless specified in policy
	all-risks	unspecified items	current value; excess may apply and limit on payment per item; may be subject to average
		specified items	current insured value
fire destroys the house			
roof, walls, floors damaged or destroyed	buildings	fire	cost of repair or reconstruction, debris clearance and professional fees
carpets, curtains, furniture destroyed	contents	fire	current value (or replacement cost)
landlord's fixtures and fittings, for which you are liable as tenant, damaged or destroyed	contents	tenant's liability	not more than set percentage (usually 10%) of sum insured; unoccupancy clause applies; some policies exclude sanitary ware and fixed glass
household linen destroyed	contents	fire	current value (even on replacement-as-new policy)
clothes and valuables destroyed or damaged	contents	fire	not more than set percentage of sum insured for any one valuable unless specified in policy
	all-risks	unspecified items	current value; excess may apply and limit on payment per item; may be subject to average
		specified items	current insured value
you have to stay in a hotel or go to lodgings because of the fire	buildings } contents	loss of rent or alternative accommodation	mostly up to 10% of both sums insured

the happening	*policy cover*		*what you get*
defective oil stove			
causes smoke damage to decorations	buildings	fire	*no cover*
causes smoke damage to furniture, curtains, clothes	contents	fire	*no cover* (unless insured on all-risks basis; excess applies)
causes smoke damage to clothes	all-risks	unspecified items	current value or cost of cleaning; excess may apply and limit on payment per item; may be subject to average
dress scorched with too hot an iron	contents	fire	*no cover* (but may get an ex gratia payment)
	all-risks	unspecified items	current value; subject to single article limit; excess may apply
a storm has damaged your property			
slates blown from roof, gutter fallen down	buildings	storm	cost of repairs; excess applies (£15 or more)
damage so bad that you have to stay in a hotel or go to lodgings	buildings	loss of rent or alternative accommodation	mostly up to 10% of sum insured
damage to furniture by rain or wind blowing in	contents	storm	current value (or replacement cost) or cost of repairs (may be deduction for betterment)
tv aerial blown off, damaging roof	buildings	breakage of aerials	cost of repairing roof *no cover* for damage to aerial
	contents	storm	cost of replacing aerial (*no cover* in some policies)
fence and front gate blown down	buildings	storm	*no cover*

water has overflowed from a tank or pipe

walls and floors stained	buildings	bursting or overflowing of tanks etc	cost of repairs; excess applies (£15 or more) unoccupancy clause applies *no cover* for damaged apparatus (e.g. the burst pipe) in some policies
furniture, clothes and household possessions stained or damaged	contents	bursting or overflowing of tanks etc	current value or cost of cleaning or repairing *no cover* for the damaged apparatus
neighbour's property damaged and you are legally liable	contents	occupier's liability	cost of repairs and damages, usually limited to a specified sum (£250,000 or more), in some policies unlimited
landlord's floor coverings or other property damaged for which you are liable as tenant	contents	tenant's liability	not more than set percentage (usually 10%) of sum insured (may be deduction for betterment); excess (£15 or more) applies; unoccupancy clause applies

an underground public service cable or pipe or drain has been damaged

water pipe connecting house to public mains cracked accidentally when digging up path	buildings	damage to underground pipes	cost of repairing the pipe
water from the cracked pipe floods into the house and ruins floors	buildings	bursting or overflowing of water pipes	cost of repair or replacement (may be deduction for betterment); excess (£15 or more) applies; unoccupancy clause applies
water damages landlord's floor coverings for which you are liable as tenant	contents	tenant's liability	not more than set percentage (usually 10%) of sum insured (may be deduction for betterment); excess (£15 or more) applies; unoccupancy clause applies
water escapes into neighbour's property and causes damage for which you are legally liable	contents	occupier's liability	cost of repairs and damages; usually limited to specified sum (£250,000 or more), in some policies unlimited

the happening	policy cover		what you get
panes of glass get broken			
glass in a window or door	buildings	breakage of fixed glass	cost of repair; in some policies, unoccupancy clause applies
glass in a bookcase or other furniture, a picture, a mirror	contents	breakage of mirrors and glass	cost of repair
glass door for which you are liable as tenant	contents	tenant's liability	not more than set percentage (usually 10%) of sum insured; unoccupancy clause applies
a washbasin, sink, bath, lavatory pan or cistern gets broken or cracked	buildings	breakage of sanitary fixtures	cost of repairs or replacement; in some policies, unoccupancy clause applies
for which you are liable as tenant	contents	tenant's liability	not more than set percentage (usually 10%) of sum insured; in some policies, unoccupancy clause applies
freezer contents un-frozen			
accidental failure of electricity supply	contents	extension for freezer	value of spoilt food
	special freezer policy		*no cover* if freezer older than specified number of years
power cut due to industrial dispute	contents	extension for freezer	value of spoilt food
	special freezer policy		*no cover:* specifically excluded

Some relevant reports in *Which?*

HW *Handyman Which?*
MW *Money Which?*
W *Which?*

● **Knowing where to turn**

builder, choosing a	HW Aug 1979
electrical work, getting done	W Aug 1980
home safety	W Mar 1979
local authority services	HW Feb 1980
plumber, finding	HW Feb 1973
refuse, disposing of	HW Feb 1980
repair services:	
electrical	W July 1979
	W July 1980
reliability	W Feb 1977
trees	HW Aug 1979
and local authority	HW Feb 1980
water	W Jan 1980
services	HW Feb 1980

● **Simple tools**

adhesives	HW May 1981
chisels	HW Nov 1975
d-i-y jobs:	
accidents	W Mar 1979
	HW Aug 1976
help with	HW Feb 1980
pros and cons	HW Nov 1977
where to buy goods	HW Feb 1979
drills:	
electric	HW Nov 1979
hand	HW Feb 1980
fixing things to walls	HW Aug 1981
hammers	HW Nov 1976
hire or buy?	HW Feb 1978
knives, trimming	HW Nov 1977
ladders	HW Feb 1981
step ladders	HW May 1978
multimeters	HW Feb 1976
nailing	HW Nov 1976
pliers, combination	HW Aug 1974
saws	HW May 1975
general purpose	HW Feb 1973
hand, for metal	HW Aug 1975
for wood, sharpening	HW May 1979
screwdrivers	HW Nov 1980
screws	HW Nov 1980
soldering irons	HW Nov 1981
spanners	HW Nov 1974
socket	HW Nov 1978
storing bits and pieces	HW Feb 1977
tool kits	HW Nov 1981
tools:	
for marking	HW Nov 1980

The Which? book of do-it-yourself gives detailed and clear instructions about maintenance and repair jobs, including decorating, woodworking, bricklaying, fixing things to walls, laying floors, installing electric circuits and fittings, repairing roofs, putting in doors and windows, metalworking, plumbing, dealing with damp, rot and woodworm.

● *Electrical emergencies*

Index

abdominal thrusts, 127, 128
abdominal wound, 135
acetic acid *see* white vinegar
acetone, 112, 116, 117
accidents, first aid after, 118 *et seq*
adaptors, 52
adhesives
– and fire risk, 85
– getting unstuck from, 98
– stains from, 111, 112, 117
aerosols, fire risk 85
airlocks
– in central heating system, 55
– in water system, 61
alcohol, not giving, 120, 129, 132
all-risks insurance, 141 *et seq*
ambulance, calling, 18, 119, 124, 128, 131, 135
AMDEA, 16
ammonia, 111, 112, 114, 116, 117, 124
amps, 31
– and appliances, 32, 37, 50, 51
– and flex, 37
– and fuses, 29, 31, 32 *et seq*, 50, 51
amyl acetate, 112
animal, trapped, 98, 99
– bites from, 122, 134
ants, dealing with, 105
appliances, electric, 16, 41 *et seq*
– and amps, 32, 37, 50, 51
– avoiding emergencies with, 52, 53
– codes of practice for, 16
– dismantling, 38, 42, 45, 46, 47, 48
– faulty, 35, 36 *et seq*, 42 *et seq*, 49, 52, 53
– and fire, 81, 83, 87, 88, 89
– servicing of, 16, 17, 41, 47
– switching off/on, 34, 36, 42, 45, 47, 49, 79, 88
– wattages of, 50, 51, 52
artificial respiration, 120, 121, 128, 129, 131, 132

average, in insurance policy, 141 *et seq*
see also under-insurance

ball valve *see* float
basins *see* washbasins
bath, 137, 144
– water supply to, 9, 12, 55
beading, window, 94, 96
bee stings, 132
beer stains, 115, 117
betterment, on insurance claim, 137, 140 *et seq*
bird
– down chimney, 99
– stains from droppings, 117
bites, from cat or dog, 122, 134
see also wound
blanket, electric, 47, 50, 89, 115, 129
bleach, 108, 112, 116, 117, 124
bleeding, control of, 119, 120, 122, 123, 130, 131, 133, 134
blisters, 124
blockages, 54 et *seq*
– in pipes, 54, 55, 57
– in sink outlet, 63 *et seq*
– at w.c., 67 *et seq*
blood stains, 113, 114, 115, 117
bonfires, 89, 90
bottle, undoing stuck, 99, 110
bottle trap, 65, 66
bottled gas, fire risk, 86, 89
breathing, stopped, 120, 121, 128, 129, 131, 132
British Gas leaflet, 10, 11
British Pest Control Association, 103
British Standard
– 3924: adhesive tape, 28
– 5423/6165: fire extinguishers, 80, 81
– 1362: fuses in plugs, 40

Avoiding back trouble
tells you about the spine and what can go wrong with it, concentrating mainly on the lower back. It advises on ways of avoiding back trouble, and for those who suffer from backache already, offers guidance on how to ease it, how to live with it and how to avoid becoming a chronic sufferer. It deals with causes of back trouble, specialist examination and treatment and gives hints on general care of the back when sitting, standing, lifting, carrying, doing housework, gardening, driving.

Avoiding heart trouble
identifies the factors which make a person more likely to develop heart trouble and describes how the various risk factors interact: cigarette smoking, raised blood pressure, high level of blood fats, stress, hereditary and dietary factors, oral contraceptives, overweight. It warns of the more serious signs and symptoms of heart trouble and, where possible, tells you what can be done about them.

Central heating
helps you to choose central heating for your home, giving details of the equipment involved—boilers, radiators, heat emitters, thermostats and other controls, warm air units, ducting—and discussing the different fuels, the importance of insulation, and the installation.

Cutting your cost of living
helps you take care of the pence—and the pounds too. It advises you on how to cut down your spending by adapting your shopping habits, how to make small savings (on food, heating, gardening) and larger ones (on travel, do-it-yourself, holidays, luxuries), giving warnings about false economies and guidance on how to take advantage of what is available free.

Earning money at home
for the person who has to stay at home and would like to make some money at the same time, the book explains what this entails in the way of organising domestic life, family and children, keeping accounts, taking out insurance, coping with tax, costing, dealing with customers, getting supplies. It suggests many activities that could be undertaken, with or without previous experience.

Extending your house
describes what is involved in having an extension built on to a house
or bungalow, explaining what has to be done, when and by whom. It
explains how the Building Regulations affect the position and design
of an extension, and how to apply for planning permission and Building
Regulations approval.

Getting a new job
is a practical guide to the steps to take from when one job ends to the
day the next one begins. The circumstances relating to unfair dismissal
are explained and the remedies available. The book defines redundancy
and lists your rights; it explains how redundancy payment is calculated
and what can be done when an employer does not pay up. It also
suggests how an employer can help a redundant employee find another
job.
The book deals with job hunting, how to apply, what to do to get an
interview and to make sure that the interview goes well. It also covers
the points to consider when being offered a job and what is involved
as an employee—the legal rights and obligations on both sides.

The legal side of buying a house
covers the procedure for buying an owner-occupied house with a
registered title in England and Wales (not Scotland) and describes the
part played by the solicitors and building society, the estate agent,
surveyor, Land Registry, insurance company and local authority. It
takes the reader step by step through a typical house purchase so that,
in many cases, he can do his own conveyancing without a solicitor; it
also deals with the legal side of selling.

Living through middle age
faces up to the physical changes and psychological difficulties for both
men and women that this stage of life may bring (some inevitable, and
some avoidable). Throughout, practical advice is given on overcoming
problems, so that you can make the most of your middle years.

The newborn baby
concentrates primarily on health and welfare in the first few weeks
after the baby is born, but also covers development in the following
months. There is advice about when and from whom to seek help.

On getting divorced

explains what steps are necessary to obtain a divorce in England or Wales, dealing with the grounds, legal advice and legal aid, preparing the petition, the procedure by post, the decrees, making arrangements about finances and property and about children.

Pregnancy month by month

goes in detail through what should happen when you are going to have a baby, mentioning some of the things that could go wrong and what can be done about them, and describing the available welfare services.

Raising the money to buy your home

gives you detailed information about the requirements of the various lenders—building society, bank, local authority, insurance company, private lender—and the procedures involved. It explains the importance of the timing of a loan and what to do when ending a mortgage early. Simple examples show how to work out what your own financial commitments are going to be throughout the period of the loan and how to use a simple calculator to work out the amount of loan outstanding at any time and, when interest rates change, what your monthly payments will be.

Securing your home

helps you keep burglars and car thieves at bay. It tells you about various means of protecting your home and safeguarding your car, the right locks to put on doors and grilles for windows. It deals with burglar alarms and installing a safe and—if the worst has happened—what to do and what not to do after a burglary, and how to make an insurance claim.

What to do when someone dies

explains about doctors' certificates, about deaths reported to the coroner and what this entails, about registering a death and getting the various certificates that may be needed afterwards. Differences between burial and cremation procedure are discussed, and the arrangements that have to be made, mainly through the undertaker, for the funeral. The book details the various national insurance benefits that may be claimed.

Where to live after retirement
discusses the points to consider when deciding whether to move or
stay put, describing the alternatives that may be available, such as
sheltered housing or a residential home.

Which? way to buy, sell and move house
takes you through all the stages of moving to another home: house
hunting, viewing, estimating costs, having a survey, making an offer,
getting a mortgage, completing, selling the present home. Practical
arrangements for the move and any necessary repairs to the new home
are dealt with, and advice is given on packing and moving possessions,
with a removal firm or on your own, and on the day of the move.

Which? way to slim
is the complete guide to losing weight and staying slim. The book
separates fact from fallacy, and gives a balanced view of essentials such
as suitable weight ranges, target weights, exercise, and the advantages
and disadvantages of the different methods of dieting. The book
highlights the dangers of being overweight and gives encouraging advice
about staying slim.

Wills and probate
is a book about wills and how to make them, and about the admin-
istration of an estate undertaken by executors without the help of a
solicitor. One section deals with intestacy and explains the difficulties
which can arise when there is no will. *Wills and probate* goes step by
step through the tasks of an executor concerned with a straightforward
will: reading the will, the valuation of the estate, payment of tax, the
steps involved in obtaining probate, the distribution of the estate in
accordance with the will, the transfer of property to the new owner,
and explains clearly the procedures involved at every stage. The book
also shows how to make a will—prepare it, sign it and have it witnessed.

All these publications are available from
Consumers' Association, Caxton Hill, Hertford SG13 7LZ
and from booksellers.

With an inward opening door, take a firm grip on the door handle, stand sideways to the door bracing the shoulders and thigh against it and then open it, just a little, to see what happens. Be prepared to slam it shut again against pressure, and make sure that the latch has caught before letting go.

An outward opening door needs a different technique. If the opening edge of the door abuts a length of wall, get behind that before pushing the door open. Where the outward opening edge is at a corner of the room, so that there is no shelter, stand sideways against the door looking towards the hinged edge and, with your back towards the opening edge, reach behind you to the handle and then push open. In this position, if there is a current of smoke or fumes coming through when the door is opened, your face and breathing will have some protection. Try a rehearsal of all this now, so that, once practised, the movements will come naturally when the emergency arises. And when you escape through fire, move as the firemen do – in a crouching position: there will be a layer of air that can be breathed at floor level.

At night, people who are asleep may be rendered unconscious by smoke and fumes before they can wake sufficiently to realise and escape. If you wake up to find the bedroom partially filled with smoke, do not sit up or leap out to stand upright: this will put your nose and mouth into a higher, and therefore hotter and more concentrated, zone of fumes. Roll out of bed on to the floor; if you need a second or two to muster your senses, turn towards the space under the bed where there may be a pocket of clearer air. Then crawl out of the room, keeping your mouth as close to the floor as possible; hold your breath if you have to rise. Hold a handkerchief over your mouth if you can, to filter some of the smoke.

If you are trapped in a house on fire, try to get to a room which is unaffected, close the door and block the space under the door to hold back the smoke. (Use something wet if possible.) Given a choice and opportunity, go to a room on the side of the main entrance or facing the road so that there is a greater chance of being seen by people outside. Stand by the window to attract attention or sit outside on the window ledge with the window closed behind you or astride the sill with the window pulled down as far as possible. Do not jump from an upper storey window unless this becomes imperative, and not if flames are coming from beneath. If the door to the room you are in is shut, it should hold the fire back for some minutes.

If you are forced to jump, do not jump facing outwards; lower yourself by your hands from the window sill to cut down the distance you have to drop. Let go of one hand and use that arm and your legs to push off from the wall as you drop. Relax as much as possible as you fall, to lessen the impact when you land.

If you are higher than a first floor window, it is unlikely that you will be able to jump down without injuring yourself. If it is absolutely necessary to jump, try to lessen the distance you have to fall by tying curtains or bedclothes together by the corners and anchoring them to a solid piece of furniture inside the room. Even if the 'rope' does not reach to the ground, it will get you nearer before having to drop.

However, it is better to wait for the firemen to come and rescue you.

Where the only way of escape is through a window, open it in preference to breaking the glass: you may be able to shut it again on leaving which will help to contain the fire. Also, it will give you some protection if you have to hang on outside waiting for rescue, and make it easier for anyone who has to come down from a higher level to get safely past the window.

If you do have to break a window to escape, use a chair leg or kick it out rather than using your bare hands. If nothing is available to use as a breaking implement, wrap something around your fist, or use your elbow if you are wearing a sleeved garment. Be ruthless and break the glass thoroughly. Spare a moment to clear or cover jagged pieces of glass: rasp the side edges with any hard object you can get hold of and cover the sill edge with some padding, such as a rug, cushion, towel, tablecloth, to avoid getting badly cut from the slivers of broken glass as you climb through.

Once you have got out, do not wander off without making it known to the firemen, your family or neighbours that you are safe, otherwise someone else's life may be needlessly jeopardised searching for you in the belief that you are still inside the burning building.